M000031366

A Gift for the Graduate

_____

NAME

CONGRATULATIONS
ON YOUR
ACCOMPLISHMENT!

*May this little book be your guide
into the power of God's promises
for your every need in life.*

_____

FROM

_____

DATE

GOD'S PROMISES®
FOR
GRADUATES

CLASS OF 2017

Compiled by Jack Countryman

God's Promises® for Graduates: Class of 2017
© 2017 by Thomas Nelson

All rights reserved. No portion of this publication may be reproduced,
stored in a retrieval system, or transmitted by any means—electronic,
mechanical, photocopy, recording, scanning, or other—except for brief quotations
in critical reviews or articles, without the prior written permission of the publisher.

Published in Nashville, Tennessee, by Thomas Nelson. Thomas Nelson is a registered trademark of
HarperCollins Christian Publishing, Inc.

God's Promises® is a registered trademark of Thomas Nelson.

Thomas Nelson titles may be purchased in bulk for educational,
business, fund-raising, or sales promotional use. For information,
please e-mail SpecialMarkets@ThomasNelson.com.

Unless otherwise noted, Scripture quotations are taken from the New King James Version®.
©1982 by Thomas Nelson. Used by permission. All rights reserved.

Scripture quotations marked NLT are taken from the *Holy Bible,* New Living Translation. © 1996,
2004, 2007, 2013 by Tyndale House Foundation. Used by permission of Tyndale House Publishers,
Inc., Carol Stream, Illinois 60188. All rights reserved.

Scripture quotations marked NIV are taken from the Holy Bible, New International Version®,
NIV®. Copyright © 1973, 1978, 1984, 2011 by Biblica, Inc.® Used by permission of Zondervan. All
rights reserved worldwide. www.zondervan.com. The "NIV" and "New International Version" are
trademarks registered in the United States Patent and Trademark Office by Biblica, Inc.®

ISBN 978-0-7180-8606-0 (navy)
ISBN 978-0-7180-9948-0 (navy CU)
ISBN 978-0-7180-8605-3 (pink)
ISBN 978-0-7180-9947-3 (pink CU)

Printed in China

17 18 19 20 21 DSC 5 4 3 2 1

TABLE OF CONTENTS

Congratulations, graduate! You've finished one journey, and now you're starting a new one. This book is a guide for the adventures ahead.

Whatever challenges you encounter, God has promised to help you. When your faith is tested or circumstances are uncertain, you can rest confident in these guarantees from God's Word. Read them. Meditate on them. Let them soak into your spirit. And then, with God as your perfect companion, every adventure of your life will be better than you've ever imagined.

The LORD your God will bless you just as He promised you.

DEUTERONOMY 15:6

WHAT TO DO
WHEN YOU NEED...

- To Make a Change (to Please God)
- Comfort
- Confidence
- Contentment
- To Make a Decision
- Discipline
- Encouragement
- Faith
- Forgiveness
- Friendship
- Guidance
- Healing
- Hope
- Humility
- Peace
- Protection
- Repentance
- To Wait on the Lord
- Wisdom

TO MAKE A CHANGE
(TO PLEASE GOD)

Therefore, if anyone is in Christ, he is a new creation; old things have passed away; behold, all things have become new.

2 CORINTHIANS 5:17

Then I will give them a heart to know Me, that I am the LORD; and they shall be My people, and I will be their God, for they shall return to Me with their whole heart.

JEREMIAH 24:7

But as many as received Him, to them He gave the right to become children of God, to those who believe in His name: who were born, not of blood, nor of the will of the flesh, nor of the will of man, but of God.

JOHN 1:12–13

"I am the true vine, and My Father is the vinedresser. Every branch in Me that does not bear fruit He takes away; and every branch that bears fruit He prunes, that it may bear more fruit. You are already clean because of the word which I have spoken to you. Abide in Me, and I in you. As the branch cannot bear fruit of itself, unless it abides in the vine, neither can you, unless you abide in Me. I am the vine, you are the branches. He who abides in Me, and I in him, bears much fruit; for without Me you can do nothing."

JOHN 15:1–5

But when the kindness and the love of God our Savior toward man appeared, not by works of righteousness which we have done, but according to His mercy He saved us, through the washing of regeneration and renewing of the Holy Spirit, whom He poured out on us abundantly through Jesus Christ our Savior.

TITUS 3:4–6

Therefore, as the elect of God, holy and beloved, put on tender mercies, kindness, humility, meekness, longsuffering.

COLOSSIANS 3:12

Therefore, my beloved, as you have always obeyed, not as in my presence only, but now much more in my absence, work out your own salvation with fear and trembling; for it is God who works in you both to will and to do for His good pleasure.

PHILIPPIANS 2:12–13

Not that I have already attained, or am already perfected; but I press on, that I may lay hold of that for which Christ Jesus has also laid hold of me. Brethren, I do not count myself to have apprehended; but one thing I do, forgetting those things which are behind and reaching forward to those things which are ahead, I press toward the goal for the prize of the upward call of God in Christ Jesus.

PHILIPPIANS 3:12–14

If indeed you have heard Him and have been taught by Him, as the truth is in Jesus: that you put off, concerning your former conduct . . . and be renewed in the spirit of your mind, and that you put on the new man which was created according to God, in true righteousness and holiness.

EPHESIANS 4:21–24

Therefore be imitators of God as dear children. And walk in love, as Christ also has loved us and given Himself for us, an offering and a sacrifice to God for a sweet-smelling aroma.

EPHESIANS 5:1–2

For if you live according to the flesh you will die; but if by the Spirit you put to death the deeds of the body, you will live. For as many as are led by the Spirit of God, these are sons of God.

ROMANS 8:13–14

I beseech you therefore, brethren, by the mercies of God, that you present your bodies a living sacrifice, holy, acceptable to God, which is your reasonable service. And do not be conformed to this world, but be transformed by the renewing of your mind, that you may prove what is that good and acceptable and perfect will of God.

ROMANS 12:1–2

COMFORT

Nevertheless I am continually with You;
You hold me by my right hand.

PSALM 73:23

Remember the word to Your servant,
Upon which You have caused me to hope.
This is my comfort in my affliction,
For Your word has given me life. . . .
I remembered Your judgments of old, O LORD,
And have comforted myself.

PSALM 119:49–50, 52

Cast your burden on the LORD,
And He shall sustain you;
He shall never permit the righteous to be moved

PSALM 55:22

"I am the good shepherd; and I know My sheep, and
am known by My own. As the Father knows Me, even so
I know the Father; and I lay down My life for the sheep."

JOHN 10:14–15

And we know that all things work together for good
to those who love God, to those who are the called
according to His purpose.

ROMANS 8:28

"And I will pray the Father, and He will give you another Helper, that He may abide with you forever."

JOHN 14:16

"Blessed are those who mourn, for they shall be comforted."

MATTHEW 5:4

Blessed be the God and Father of our Lord Jesus Christ, the Father of mercies and God of all comfort, who comforts us in all our tribulation, that we may be able to comfort those who are in any trouble, with the comfort with which we ourselves are comforted by God.

2 CORINTHIANS 1:3–4

For our light affliction, which is but for a moment, is working for us a far more exceeding and eternal weight of glory, while we do not look at the things which are seen, but at the things which are not seen. For the things which are seen are temporary, but the things which are not seen are eternal.

2 CORINTHIANS 4:17–18

O LORD, You have searched me and known me.
You know my sitting down and my rising up;
You understand my thought afar off.
You comprehend my path and my lying down,
And are acquainted with all my ways.

PSALM 139:1–3

He said to me, "My grace is sufficient for you, for My strength is made perfect in weakness." Therefore most gladly I will rather boast in my infirmities, that the power of Christ may rest upon me. Therefore I take pleasure in infirmities, in reproaches, in needs, in persecutions, in distresses, for Christ's sake. For when I am weak, then I am strong.

2 CORINTHIANS 12:9–10

"Come to Me, all you who labor and are heavy laden, and I will give you rest."

MATTHEW 11:28

WHAT TO DO WHEN YOU NEED . . .
CONFIDENCE

Let us therefore come boldly to the throne of grace, that we may obtain mercy and find grace to help in time of need.

HEBREWS 4:16

Therefore do not cast away your confidence, which has great reward. For you have need of endurance, so that after you have done the will of God, you may receive the promise.

HEBREWS 10:35–36

The LORD is my helper;
I will not fear.
What can man do to me?

HEBREWS 13:6

For God has not given us a spirit of fear, but of power and of love and of a sound mind.

2 TIMOTHY 1:7

Beloved, if our heart does not condemn us, we have confidence toward God. And whatever we ask we receive from Him, because we keep His commandments and do those things that are pleasing in His sight.

1 JOHN 3:21–22

Blessed is the man who trusts in the LORD,
And whose hope is the LORD.

JEREMIAH 17:7

Do not be afraid of sudden terror,
Nor of trouble from the wicked when it comes;
For the LORD will be your confidence,
And will keep your foot from being caught.

PROVERBS 3:25–26

Being confident of this very thing, that He who has begun a good work in you will complete it until the day of Jesus Christ.

PHILIPPIANS 1:6

Finally, my brethren, be strong in the Lord and in the power of His might. Put on the whole armor of God, that you may be able to stand against the wiles of the devil.

EPHESIANS 6:10–11

CONTENTMENT

Let your conduct be without covetousness; be content with such things as you have. For He Himself has said, "I will never leave you nor forsake you." So we may boldly say:

"The LORD is my helper; I will not fear.
What can man do to me?"

HEBREWS 13:5–6

Not that I speak in regard to need, for I have learned in whatever state I am, to be content: I know how to be abased, and I know how to abound. Everywhere and in all things I have learned both to be full and to be hungry, both to abound and to suffer need. I can do all things through Christ who strengthens me.

PHILIPPIANS 4:11–13

The fear of the LORD leads to life,
And he who has it will abide in satisfaction;
He will not be visited with evil.

PROVERBS 19:23

"Do not lay up for yourselves treasures on earth, where moth and rust destroy and where thieves break in and steal; but lay up for yourselves treasures in heaven, where neither moth nor rust destroys and where thieves do not break in and steal. For where your treasure is, there your heart will be also."

MATTHEW 6:19–21

How much better to get wisdom than gold!
And to get understanding is to be chosen rather than silver.

PROVERBS 16:16

"But seek first the kingdom of God and His righteousness, and all these things shall be added to you."

MATTHEW 6:33

"Are not two sparrows sold for a copper coin? And not one of them falls to the ground apart from your Father's will. But the very hairs of your head are all numbered. Do not fear therefore; you are of more value than many sparrows."

MATTHEW 10:29–31

TO MAKE A DECISION

The fear of the LORD is the beginning of wisdom;
A good understanding have all those who do His
commandments.

PSALM 111:10

I beseech you therefore, brethren, by the mercies of
God, that you present your bodies a living sacrifice, holy,
acceptable to God, which is your reasonable service. And
do not be conformed to this world, but be transformed
by the renewing of your mind, that you may prove what
is that good and acceptable and perfect will of God.

ROMANS 12:1–2

Commit your works to the LORD,
And your thoughts will be established.

PROVERBS 16:3

Trust in the LORD with all your heart,
And lean not on your own understanding;
In all your ways acknowledge Him,
And He shall direct your paths.

PROVERBS 3:5–6

I will instruct you and teach you in the way you
should go;
I will guide you with My eye.

PSALM 32:8

Be anxious for nothing, but in everything by prayer and supplication, with thanksgiving, let your requests be made known to God; and the peace of God, which surpasses all understanding, will guard your hearts and minds through Christ Jesus.

PHILIPPIANS 4:6–7

Blessed is the man
Who walks not in the counsel of the ungodly. . .
But his delight is in the law of the LORD,
And in His law he meditates day and night.

PSALM 1:1–2

DISCIPLINE

Indeed it was for my own peace
That I had great bitterness;
But You have lovingly delivered my soul from the pit
of corruption,
For You have cast all my sins behind Your back.

ISAIAH 38:17

Exercise yourself toward godliness. For bodily exercise profits a little, but godliness is profitable for all things, having promise of the life that now is and of that which is to come.

1 TIMOTHY 4:7–8

But if we hope for what we do not see, we eagerly wait for it with perseverance. Likewise the Spirit also helps us in our weaknesses. For we do not know what we should pray for as we ought, but the Spirit Himself makes intercession for us with groanings which cannot be uttered.

ROMANS 8:25–26

Do you not know that those who run in a race all run, but one receives the prize? Run in such a way that you may obtain it. . . . Therefore I run thus: not with uncertainty. Thus I fight: not as one who beats the air. But I discipline my body and bring it into subjection, lest, when I have preached to others, I myself should become disqualified.

1 CORINTHIANS 9:24, 26–27

Now no chastening seems to be joyful for the present, but painful; nevertheless, afterward it yields the peaceable fruit of righteousness to those who have been trained by it.

Hebrews 12:11

You should know in your heart that as a man chastens his son, so the Lord your God chastens you.

Deuteronomy 8:5

ENCOURAGEMENT

Wait on the LORD;
Be of good courage,
And He shall strengthen your heart;
Wait, I say, on the LORD!

PSALM 27:14

But we all, with unveiled face, beholding as in a mirror the glory of the Lord, are being transformed into the same image from glory to glory, just as by the Spirit of the Lord. Therefore, since we have this ministry, as we have received mercy, we do not lose heart.

2 CORINTHIANS 3:18–4:1

"And God will wipe away every tear from their eyes; there shall be no more death, nor sorrow, nor crying. There shall be no more pain, for the former things have passed away."

Then He who sat on the throne said, "Behold, I make all things new." And He said to me, "Write, for these words are true and faithful." And He said to me, "It is done! I am the Alpha and the Omega, the Beginning and the End. I will give of the fountain of the water of life freely to him who thirsts. He who overcomes shall inherit all things, and I will be his God and he shall be My son."

REVELATION 21:4–7

And let us not grow weary while doing good, for in due season we shall reap if we do not lose heart.

GALATIANS 6:9

Be anxious for nothing, but in everything by prayer and supplication, with thanksgiving, let your requests be made known to God; and the peace of God, which surpasses all understanding, will guard your hearts and minds through Christ Jesus.

PHILIPPIANS 4:6–7

FAITH

Be strong and of good courage; do not be afraid, nor be dismayed, for the LORD your God is with you wherever you go.

JOSHUA 1:9

In this you greatly rejoice, though now for a little while, if need be, you have been grieved by various trials, that the genuineness of your faith, being much more precious than gold that perishes, though it is tested by fire, may be found to praise, honor, and glory at the revelation of Jesus Christ.

1 PETER 1:6–7

For in it the righteousness of God is revealed from faith to faith; as it is written, "The just shall live by faith."

ROMANS 1:17

So then faith comes by hearing, and hearing by the word of God.

ROMANS 10:17

So the Lord said, "If you have faith as a mustard seed, you can say to this mulberry tree, 'Be pulled up by the roots and be planted in the sea,' and it would obey you."

LUKE 17:6

As you therefore have received Christ Jesus the
Lord, so walk in Him, rooted and built up in Him
and established in the faith, as you have been taught,
abounding in it with thanksgiving.

COLOSSIANS 2:6–7

For by grace you have been saved through faith, and
that not of yourselves; it is the gift of God, not of works,
lest anyone should boast.

EPHESIANS 2:8–9

My brethren, count it all joy when you fall into
various trials, knowing that the testing of your faith
produces patience.

JAMES 1:2–3

Fight the good fight of faith, lay hold on eternal life,
to which you were also called and have confessed the
good confession in the presence of many witnesses.

1 TIMOTHY 6:12

Fear not, for I am with you;
Be not dismayed, for I am your God.
I will strengthen you,
Yes, I will help you,
I will uphold you with My righteous right hand.

ISAIAH 41:10

FORGIVENESS

If we confess our sins, He is faithful and just to forgive us our sins and to cleanse us from all unrighteousness.

1 JOHN 1:9

My little children, these things I write to you, so that you may not sin. And if anyone sins, we have an Advocate with the Father, Jesus Christ the righteous. And He Himself is the propitiation for our sins, and not for ours only but also for the whole world.

1 JOHN 2:1–2

Therefore, as the elect of God, holy and beloved, put on tender mercies, kindness, humility, meekness, longsuffering; bearing with one another, and forgiving one another, if anyone has a complaint against another; even as Christ forgave you, so you also must do.

COLOSSIANS 3:12–13

Seek the LORD while He may be found,
Call upon Him while He is near.
Let the wicked forsake his way,
And the unrighteous man his thoughts;
Let him return to the LORD,
And He will have mercy on him;
And to our God,
For He will abundantly pardon.

ISAIAH 55:6–7

In Him we have redemption through His blood, the forgiveness of sins, according to the riches of His grace which He made to abound toward us in all wisdom and prudence.

EPHESIANS 1:7–8

"Come now, and let us reason together,"
Says the LORD,
"Though your sins are like scarlet,
They shall be as white as snow;
Though they are red like crimson,
They shall be as wool."

ISAIAH 1:18

There is therefore now no condemnation to those who are in Christ Jesus, who do not walk according to the flesh, but according to the Spirit. For the law of the Spirit of life in Christ Jesus has made me free from the law of sin and death.

ROMANS 8:1–2

FRIENDSHIP

But above all these things put on love, which is the
bond of perfection.
COLOSSIANS 3:14

A friend loves at all times,
And a brother is born for adversity.
PROVERBS 17:17

Now may the God of patience and comfort grant
you to be like-minded toward one another, according
to Christ Jesus, that you may with one mind and one
mouth glorify the God and Father of our Lord Jesus
Christ. Therefore receive one another, just as Christ also
received us, to the glory of God.
ROMANS 15:5–7

And my God shall supply all your need according to
His riches in glory by Christ Jesus.
PHILIPPIANS 4:19

Ointment and perfume delight the heart,
And the sweetness of a man's friend gives delight by
hearty counsel. PROVERBS 27:9

You are My friends if you do whatever I command you. No
longer do I call you servants, for a servant does not know what
his master is doing; but I have called you friends, for all things
that I heard from My Father I have made known to you.
JOHN 15:14–15

GUIDANCE

If any of you lacks wisdom, let him ask of God, who gives to all liberally and without reproach, and it will be given to him. But let him ask in faith, with no doubting, for he who doubts is like a wave of the sea driven and tossed by the wind.

JAMES 1:5–6

I will lift up my eyes to the hills—
From whence comes my help?
My help comes from the LORD,
Who made heaven and earth.

PSALM 121:1–2

And the LORD, He is the One who goes before you. He will be with you, He will not leave you nor forsake you; do not fear nor be dismayed.

DEUTERONOMY 31:8

The humble He guides in justice,
And the humble He teaches His way.

PSALM 25:9

"However, when He, the Spirit of truth, has come, He will guide you into all truth; for He will not speak on His own authority, but whatever He hears He will speak; and He will tell you things to come."

JOHN 16:13

The steps of a good man are ordered by the LORD,
And He delights in his way.

PSALM 37:23

O LORD, I know the way of man is not in himself;
It is not in man who walks to direct his own steps.

JEREMIAH 10:23

Your ears shall hear a word behind you, saying,
"This is the way, walk in it,"
Whenever you turn to the right hand
Or whenever you turn to the left.

ISAIAH 30:21

Now may the Lord direct your hearts into the love of
God and into the patience of Christ.

2 THESSALONIANS 3:5

HEALING

Is anyone among you suffering? Let him pray. Is anyone cheerful? Let him sing psalms. Is anyone among you sick? Let him call for the elders of the church, and let them pray over him, anointing him with oil in the name of the Lord. And the prayer of faith will save the sick, and the Lord will raise him up. And if he has committed sins, he will be forgiven. Confess your trespasses to one another, and pray for one another, that you may be healed. The effective, fervent prayer of a righteous man avails much.

JAMES 5:13–16

So you shall serve the LORD your God, and He will bless your bread and your water. And I will take sickness away from the midst of you. No one shall suffer miscarriage or be barren in your land; I will fulfill the number of your days.

EXODUS 23:25–26

But to you who fear My name
The Sun of Righteousness shall arise
With healing in His wings;
And you shall go out
And grow fat like stall-fed calves.

MALACHI 4:2

Bless the LORD, O my soul,
And forget not all His benefits:
Who forgives all your iniquities,
Who heals all your diseases.

PSALM 103:2–3

O LORD my God, I cried out to You,
And You healed me.

PSALM 30:2

Many are the afflictions of the righteous,
But the LORD delivers him out of them all.

PSALM 34:19

Who Himself bore our sins in His own body on the tree, that we, having died to sins, might live for righteousness—by whose stripes you were healed.

1 PETER 2:24

HOPE

No temptation has overtaken you except such as is common to man; but God is faithful, who will not allow you to be tempted beyond what you are able, but with the temptation will also make the way of escape, that you may be able to bear it.

1 Corinthians 10:13

And God is able to make all grace abound toward you, that you, always having all sufficiency in all things, may have an abundance for every good work.

2 Corinthians 9:8

Why are you cast down, O my soul?
And why are you disquieted within me?
Hope in God, for I shall yet praise Him
For the help of His countenance.

Psalm 42:5

For I know the thoughts that I think toward you, says the Lord, thoughts of peace and not of evil, to give you a future and a hope.

Jeremiah 29:11

Blessed be the God and Father of our Lord Jesus Christ, who according to His abundant mercy has begotten us again to a living hope through the resurrection of Jesus Christ from the dead.

1 PETER 1:3

Have you not known?
Have you not heard?
The everlasting God, the LORD,
The Creator of the ends of the earth,
Neither faints nor is weary.
His understanding is unsearchable.
He gives power to the weak,
And to those who have no might He increases strength.
Even the youths shall faint and be weary,
And the young men shall utterly fall,
But those who wait on the LORD
Shall renew their strength;
They shall mount up with wings like eagles,
They shall run and not be weary,
They shall walk and not faint.

ISAIAH 40:28–31

Happy is he who has the God of Jacob for his help,
Whose hope is in the LORD his God,
Who made heaven and earth,
The sea, and all that is in them;
Who keeps truth forever.

PSALM 146:5–6

To them God willed to make known what are the riches of the glory of this mystery among the Gentiles: which is Christ in you, the hope of glory.

COLOSSIANS 1:27

The LORD takes pleasure in those who fear Him, In those who hope in His mercy.

PSALM 147:11

HUMILITY

The fear of the Lord is the instruction of wisdom,
And before honor is humility

PROVERBS 15:33

By humility and the fear of the LORD
Are riches and honor and life.

PROVERBS 22:4

Let another man praise you, and not your own mouth;
A stranger, and not your own lips.

PROVERBS 27:2

"For all those things My hand has made,
And all those things exist,"
Says the LORD.
"But on this one will I look:
On him who is poor and of a contrite spirit,
And who trembles at My word."

ISAIAH 66:2

For I say, through the grace given to me, to everyone
who is among you, not to think of himself more highly
than he ought to think, but to think soberly, as God has
dealt to each one a measure of faith.

ROMANS 12:3

"For whoever exalts himself will be humbled, and he who humbles himself will be exalted."

LUKE 14:11

Therefore humble yourselves under the mighty hand of God, that He may exalt you in due time, casting all your care upon Him, for He cares for you.

1 PETER 5:6–7

PEACE

And let the peace of God rule in your hearts, to which also you were called in one body; and be thankful.

COLOSSIANS 3:15

Let your gentleness be known to all men. The Lord is at hand. Be anxious for nothing, but in everything by prayer and supplication, with thanksgiving, let your requests be made known to God; and the peace of God, which surpasses all understanding, will guard your hearts and minds through Christ Jesus.

PHILIPPIANS 4:5–7

I will both lie down in peace, and sleep;
For You alone, O LORD, make me dwell in safety.

PSALM 4:8

"These things I have spoken to you, that in Me you may have peace. In the world you will have tribulation; but be of good cheer, I have overcome the world."

JOHN 16:33

You will keep him in perfect peace,
Whose mind is stayed on You,
Because he trusts in You.
Trust in the LORD forever,
For in YAH, the LORD, is everlasting strength.

ISAIAH 26:3–4

I will hear what God the LORD will speak,
For He will speak peace
To His people and to His saints;
But let them not turn back to folly.

PSALM 85:8

When a man's ways please the LORD,
He makes even his enemies to be at peace with him.

PROVERBS 16:7

"Peace I leave with you, My peace I give to you; not as the world gives do I give to you. Let not your heart be troubled, neither let it be afraid."

JOHN 14:27

Depart from evil and do good;
Seek peace and pursue it.
The eyes of the LORD are on the righteous,
And His ears are open to their cry.

PSALM 34:14–15

The LORD bless you and keep you;
The LORD make His face shine upon you,
And be gracious to you;
The LORD lift up His countenance upon you,
And give you peace.

NUMBERS 6:24–26

PROTECTION

My defense is of God,
Who saves the upright in heart.

PSALM 7:10

The angel of the LORD encamps all around those who
    fear Him,
And delivers them.
Oh, taste and see that the LORD is good;
Blessed is the man who trusts in Him!

PSALM 34:7–8

Because you have made the LORD, who is my refuge,
Even the Most High, your dwelling place,
No evil shall befall you,
Nor shall any plague come near your dwelling;
For He shall give His angels charge over you,
To keep you in all your ways.

PSALM 91:9–11

When you lie down, you will not be afraid;
Yes, you will lie down and your sleep will be sweet.
Do not be afraid of sudden terror,
Nor of trouble from the wicked when it comes;
For the LORD will be your confidence,
And will keep your foot from being caught.

PROVERBS 3:24–26

When you pass through the waters, I will be with you;
And through the rivers, they shall not overflow you.
When you walk through the fire, you shall not be
  burned,
Nor shall the flame scorch you.

ISAIAH 43:2

"I will make you to this people a fortified bronze wall;
And they will fight against you,
But they shall not prevail against you;
For I am with you to save you
And deliver you," says the LORD.
"I will deliver you from the hand of the wicked,
And I will redeem you from the grip of the terrible."

JEREMIAH 15:20–21

Have I not commanded you? Be strong and of good
courage; do not be afraid, nor be dismayed, for the LORD
your God is with you wherever you go.

JOSHUA 1:9

REPENTANCE

If My people who are called by My name will humble themselves, and pray and seek My face, and turn from their wicked ways, then I will hear from heaven, and will forgive their sin and heal their land.

2 CHRONICLES 7:14

Jesus answered and said to them, "Those who are well have no need of a physician, but those who are sick. I have not come to call the righteous, but sinners, to repentance."

LUKE 5:31–32

Seek the LORD while He may be found,
Call upon Him while He is near.
Let the wicked forsake his way,
And the unrighteous man his thoughts;
Let him return to the LORD,
And He will have mercy on him;
And to our God,
For He will abundantly pardon.

ISAIAH 55:6–7

I acknowledged my sin to You,
And my iniquity I have not hidden.
I said, "I will confess my transgressions to the LORD,"
And You forgave the iniquity of my sin.

PSALM 32:5

He who covers his sins will not prosper,
But whoever confesses and forsakes them will have mercy.

PROVERBS 28:13

For godly sorrow produces repentance leading to salvation, not to be regretted.

2 CORINTHIANS 7:10

But, beloved, do not forget this one thing, that with the Lord one day is as a thousand years, and a thousand years as one day. The Lord is not slack concerning His promise, as some count slackness, but is longsuffering toward us, not willing that any should perish but that all should come to repentance.

2 PETER 3:8–9

TO WAIT ON THE LORD

Therefore humble yourselves under the mighty hand of God, that He may exalt you in due time, casting all your care upon Him, for He cares for you.

1 PETER 5:6–7

Seeing then that we have a great High Priest who has passed through the heavens, Jesus the Son of God, let us hold fast our confession. For we do not have a High Priest who cannot sympathize with our weaknesses, but was in all points tempted as we are, yet without sin. Let us therefore come boldly to the throne of grace, that we may obtain mercy and find grace to help in time of need.

HEBREWS 4:14–16

The eyes of the LORD are on the righteous,
And His ears are open to their cry.

PSALM 34:15

Behold, the eye of the LORD is on those who fear Him,
On those who hope in His mercy. . . .
Our soul waits for the LORD;
He is our help and our shield.
For our heart shall rejoice in Him,
Because we have trusted in His holy name.

PSALM 33:18, 20–21

Call upon Me in the day of trouble;
I will deliver you, and you shall glorify Me.

PSALM 50:15

"Come to Me, all you who labor and are heavy laden,
and I will give you rest. Take My yoke upon you and
learn from Me, for I am gentle and lowly in heart, and
you will find rest for your souls. For My yoke is easy and
My burden is light."

MATTHEW 11:28–30

Be still, and know that I am God.

PSALM 46:10

WISDOM

If any of you lacks wisdom, let him ask of God, who gives to all liberally and without reproach, and it will be given to him.

JAMES 1:5

The fear of the LORD is the beginning of wisdom;
A good understanding have all those who do His
   commandments.
His praise endures forever.

PSALM 111:10

Now we have received, not the spirit of the world, but the Spirit who is from God, that we might know the things that have been freely given to us by God. These things we also speak, not in words which man's wisdom teaches, comparing spiritual things with spiritual.

1 CORINTHIANS 2:12–13

How much better to get wisdom than gold!
And to get understanding is to be chosen rather than silver.

PROVERBS 16:16

Happy is the man who finds wisdom,
And the man who gains understanding;
For her proceeds are better than the profits of silver,
And her gain than fine gold.

PROVERBS 3:13–14

He gives wisdom to the wise
And knowledge to those who have understanding.

DANIEL 2:21

For the LORD gives wisdom;
From His mouth come knowledge and understanding.

PROVERBS 2:6

"I will give you a mouth and wisdom which all your adversaries will not be able to contradict or resist."

LUKE 21:15

WHAT TO DO
WHEN YOU FEEL...

- Angry
- Anxiety and Worry
- Depressed
- Discouraged
- Doubt
- Fear
- Guilty
- Lonely

WHAT TO DO WHEN YOU FEEL . . .
ANGRY

So then, my beloved brethren, let every man be swift to hear, slow to speak, slow to wrath; for the wrath of man does not produce the righteousness of God.

JAMES 1:19–20

A soft answer turns away wrath,
But a harsh word stirs up anger.

PROVERBS 15:1

But now you yourselves are to put off all these: anger, wrath, malice, blasphemy, filthy language out of your mouth.

COLOSSIANS 3:8

A fool vents all his feelings,
But a wise man holds them back.

PROVERBS 29:11

"Be angry, and do not sin": do not let the sun go down on your wrath, nor give place to the devil.

EPHESIANS 4:26–27

Let all bitterness, wrath, anger, clamor, and evil speaking be put away from you, with all malice. And be kind to one another, tenderhearted, forgiving one another, even as God in Christ forgave you.

EPHESIANS 4:31–32

Be angry, and do not sin.
Meditate within your heart on your bed, and be still.
Offer the sacrifices of righteousness,
And put your trust in the LORD.

PSALM 4:4–5

He who has knowledge spares his words,
And a man of understanding is of a calm spirit.

PROVERBS 17:27

ANXIETY AND WORRY

"Therefore I say to you, do not worry about your life, what you will eat or what you will drink; nor about your body, what you will put on. Is not life more than food and the body more than clothing? Look at the birds of the air, for they neither sow nor reap nor gather into barns; yet your heavenly Father feeds them. Are you not of more value than they?"

MATTHEW 6:25–26

Be anxious for nothing, but in everything by prayer and supplication, with thanksgiving, let your requests be made known to God; and the peace of God, which surpasses all understanding, will guard your hearts and minds through Christ Jesus.

PHILIPPIANS 4:6–7

I sought the LORD, and He heard me,
And delivered me from all my fears.

PSALM 34:4

Therefore humble yourselves under the mighty hand of God, that He may exalt you in due time, casting all your care upon Him, for He cares for you.

1 PETER 5:6–7

Trust in Him at all times, you people;
Pour out your heart before Him;
God is a refuge for us.

PSALM 62:8

Anxiety in the heart of man causes depression,
But a good word makes it glad.

PROVERBS 12:25

Why are you cast down, O my soul?
And why are you disquieted within me?
Hope in God, for I shall yet praise Him
For the help of His countenance.
O my God, my soul is cast down within me;
Therefore I will remember You from the land of the Jordan,
And from the heights of Hermon,
From the Hill Mizar.

PSALM 42:5–6

And we know that all things work together for good
to those who love God, to those who are the called
according to His purpose.

ROMANS 8:28

The LORD is my light and my salvation;
Whom shall I fear?
The LORD is the strength of my life;
Of whom shall I be afraid?

PSALM 27:1

God is our refuge and strength,
A very present help in trouble.

PSALM 46:1

Blessed is the man who trusts in the LORD,
And whose hope is the LORD.
For he shall be like a tree planted by the waters,
Which spreads out its roots by the river,
And will not fear when heat comes;
But its leaf will be green,
And will not be anxious in the year of drought,
Nor will cease from yielding fruit.

JEREMIAH 17:7–8

DEPRESSED

My soul still remembers
And sinks within me.
This I recall to my mind,
Therefore I have hope.
Through the LORD's mercies we are not consumed.
Because His compassions fail not.
They are new every morning;
Great is Your faithfulness.

LAMENTATIONS 3:20–23

As for me, I will call upon God,
And the LORD shall save me.
Evening and morning and at noon
I will pray, and cry aloud,
And He shall hear my voice.
He has redeemed my soul in peace from the battle
    that was against me,
For there were many against me.

PSALM 55:16–18

I will bless the LORD who has given me counsel;
My heart also instructs me in the night seasons.
I have set the LORD always before me;
Because He is at my right hand I shall not be moved.

PSALM 16:7–8

Trust in the LORD, and do good;
Dwell in the land, and feed on His faithfulness.
Delight yourself also in the LORD,
And He shall give you the desires of your heart.
Commit your way to the LORD,
Trust also in Him,
And He shall bring it to pass.
He shall bring forth your righteousness as the light,
And your justice as the noonday.

PSALM 37:3–6

Why are you cast down, O my soul?
And why are you disquieted within me?
Hope in God;
For I shall yet praise Him,
The help of my countenance and my God.

PSALM 42:11

My flesh and my heart fail;
But God is the strength of my heart and my portion forever.

PSALM 73:26

Trust in the LORD with all your heart,
And lean not on your own understanding;
In all your ways acknowledge Him,
And He shall direct your paths.

PROVERBS 3:5–6

DISCOURAGED

Cast your burden on the LORD,
And He shall sustain you;
He shall never permit the righteous to be moved.

PSALM 55:22

In the day when I cried out, You answered me,
And made me bold with strength in my soul.

PSALM 138:3

Have I not commanded you? Be strong and of good
courage; do not be afraid, nor be dismayed, for the LORD
your God is with you wherever you go.

JOSHUA 1:9

And the LORD, He is the One who goes before you. He
will be with you, He will not leave you nor forsake you;
do not fear nor be dismayed.

DEUTERONOMY 31:8

Fight the good fight of faith, lay hold on eternal life,
to which you were also called and have confessed the
good confession in the presence of many witnesses.

1 TIMOTHY 6:12

Let us hold fast the confession of our hope without
wavering, for He who promised is faithful.

HEBREWS 10:23

The Lord is my strength and my shield;
My heart trusted in Him, and I am helped;
Therefore my heart greatly rejoices,
And with my song I will praise Him.

PSALM 28:7

Brethren, I do not count myself to have apprehended; but one thing I do, forgetting those things which are behind and reaching forward to those things which are ahead, I press toward the goal for the prize of the upward call of God in Christ Jesus.

PHILIPPIANS 3:13–14

Then you will prosper, if you take care to fulfill the statutes and judgments with which the LORD charged Moses concerning Israel. Be strong and of good courage; do not fear nor be dismayed.

1 CHRONICLES 22:13

DOUBT

But He said to them, "Why are you fearful, O you of little faith?" Then He arose and rebuked the winds and the sea, and there was a great calm.

MATTHEW 8:26

"Let not your heart be troubled; you believe in God, believe also in Me."

JOHN 14:1

Now to Him who is able to establish you according to my gospel and the preaching of Jesus Christ, according to the revelation of the mystery kept secret since the world began but now made manifest, and by the prophetic Scriptures made known to all nations, according to the commandment of the everlasting God, for obedience to the faith—to God, alone wise, be glory through Jesus Christ forever. Amen.

ROMANS 16:25–27

But Zion said, "The LORD has forsaken me,
And my Lord has forgotten me."
"Can a woman forget her nursing child,
And not have compassion on the son of her womb?
Surely they may forget,
Yet I will not forget you," . . . says the LORD.

ISAIAH 49:14–15,18

Forever, O LORD,
Your word is settled in heaven.

PSALM 119:89

Blessed is the man
Who walks not in the counsel of the ungodly,
Nor stands in the path of sinners,
Nor sits in the seat of the scornful;
But his delight is in the law of the LORD,
And in His law he meditates day and night.
He shall be like a tree
Planted by the rivers of water,
That brings forth its fruit in its season,
Whose leaf also shall not wither;
And whatever he does shall prosper.

PSALM 1:1–3

The grass withers, the flower fades,
But the word of our God stands forever.

ISAIAH 40:8

But you, beloved, building yourselves up on your most holy faith, praying in the Holy Spirit, keep yourselves in the love of God, looking for the mercy of our Lord Jesus Christ unto eternal life.

JUDE VV. 20–21

For whatever things were written before were written for our learning, that we through the patience and comfort of the Scriptures might have hope.

ROMANS 15:4

For the word of God is living and powerful, and sharper than any two-edged sword, piercing even to the division of soul and spirit, and of joints and marrow, and is a discerner of the thoughts and intents of the heart.

HEBREWS 4:12

FEAR

Fear not, for I am with you;
Be not dismayed, for I am your God.
I will strengthen you,
Yes, I will help you,
I will uphold you with My righteous right hand.

ISAIAH 41:10

But now, thus says the LORD, who created you, O Jacob,
And He who formed you, O Israel:
"Fear not, for I have redeemed you;
I have called you by your name;
You are Mine.
When you pass through the waters, I will be with you;
And through the rivers, they shall not overflow you.
When you walk through the fire, you shall not be burned,
Nor shall the flame scorch you."

ISAIAH 43:1–2

For you did not receive the spirit of bondage again to
fear, but you received the Spirit of adoption by whom
we cry out, "Abba, Father." The Spirit Himself bears
witness with our spirit that we are children of God.

ROMANS 8:15–16

I sought the LORD, and He heard me,
And delivered me from all my fears.

PSALM 34:4

The LORD is my light and my salvation;
Whom shall I fear?
The LORD is the strength of my life;
Of whom shall I be afraid?

PSALM 27:1

And we know that all things work together for good
to those who love God, to those who are the called
according to His purpose.

ROMANS 8:28

Yea, though I walk through the valley of the shadow
   of death,
I will fear no evil; for You are with me;
Your rod and Your staff, they comfort me.

PSALM 23:4

Whenever I am afraid, I will trust in You.
In God (I will praise His word),
In God I have put my trust; I will not fear.
What can flesh do to me?

PSALM 56:3–4

But whoever listens to me will dwell safely,
And will be secure, without fear of evil.

PROVERBS 1:33

There is no fear in love; but perfect love casts out fear,
because fear involves torment. But he who fears has not
been made perfect in love.

1 JOHN 4:18

GUILTY

Confess your trespasses to one another, and pray for one another, that you may be healed.

JAMES 5:16

There is therefore now no condemnation to those who are in Christ Jesus, who do not walk according to the flesh, but according to the Spirit. For the law of the Spirit of life in Christ Jesus has made me free from the law of sin and death.

ROMANS 8:1–2

If we confess our sins, He is faithful and just to forgive us our sins and to cleanse us from all unrighteousness.

1 JOHN 1:9

"Therefore if the Son makes you free, you shall be free indeed."

JOHN 8:36

I, even I, am He who blots out your transgressions for
    My own sake;
And I will not remember your sins.

ISAIAH 43:25

Draw near to God and He will draw near to you. . . . Humble yourselves in the sight of the Lord, and He will lift you up.

JAMES 4:8, 10

I acknowledged my sin to You,
And my iniquity I have not hidden.
I said, "I will confess my transgressions to the LORD,"
And You forgave the iniquity of my sin.

PSALM 32:5

"Nevertheless I tell you the truth. It is to your advantage that I go away; for if I do not go away, the Helper will not come to you; but if I depart, I will send Him to you. And when He has come, He will convict the world of sin, and of righteousness, and of judgment."

JOHN 16:7–8

The son shall not bear the guilt of the father, nor the father bear the guilt of the son. The righteousness of the righteous shall be upon himself.

EZEKIEL 18:20

LONELY

For He Himself has said, "I will never leave you nor forsake you."

HEBREWS 13:5

I waited patiently for the LORD;
And He inclined to me,
And heard my cry.
He also brought me up out of a horrible pit,
Out of the miry clay,
And set my feet upon a rock,
And established my steps.
He has put a new song in my mouth—
Praise to our God;
Many will see it and fear,
And will trust in the LORD.

PSALM 40:1–3

Jesus answered and said to him, "If anyone loves Me, he will keep My word; and My Father will love him, and We will come to him and make Our home with him."

JOHN 14:23

A father of the fatherless, a defender of widows,
Is God in His holy habitation.
God sets the solitary in families;
He brings out those who are bound into prosperity.

PSALM 68:5–6

Fear not, for I am with you;
Be not dismayed, for I am your God.
I will strengthen you,
Yes, I will help you,
I will uphold you with My righteous right hand.

ISAIAH 41:10

Where can I go from Your Spirit?
Or where can I flee from Your presence?
If I ascend into heaven, You are there;
If I make my bed in hell, behold, You are there.
If I take the wings of the morning,
And dwell in the uttermost parts of the sea,
Even there Your hand shall lead me,
And Your right hand shall hold me.
If I say, "Surely the darkness shall fall on me,"
Even the night shall be light about me;
Indeed, the darkness shall not hide from You,
But the night shines as the day;
The darkness and the light are both alike to You.

PSALM 139:7–12

"Come to Me, all you who labor and are heavy laden,
and I will give you rest. Take My yoke upon you and
learn from Me, for I am gentle and lowly in heart, and
you will find rest for your souls. For My yoke is easy and
My burden is light."

MATTHEW 11:28–30

WHAT THE BIBLE
HAS TO SAY ABOUT...

- Addiction
- Alienation from God
- Your Conscience
- Foul Language
- Hate
- Holiness
- The Holy Spirit
- Leading Someone to Christ
- Love of God
- Love of Others
- Marriage
- Money
- Obedience
- Overcoming Evil

WHAT THE BIBLE HAS TO SAY ABOUT . . .
ADDICTION

Therefore, brethren, we are debtors—not to the flesh, to live according to the flesh. For if you live according to the flesh you will die; but if by the Spirit you put to death the deeds of the body, you will live. For as many as are led by the Spirit of God, these are sons of God. For you did not receive the spirit of bondage again to fear, but you received the Spirit of adoption by whom we cry out, "Abba, Father."

ROMANS 8:12–15

Yet in all these things we are more than conquerors through Him who loved us.

ROMANS 8:37

Now to Him who is able to do exceedingly abundantly above all that we ask or think, according to the power that works in us, to Him be glory in the church by Christ Jesus to all generations, forever and ever. Amen.

EPHESIANS 3:20–21

Or do you not know that your body is the temple of the Holy Spirit who is in you, whom you have from God, and you are not your own? For you were bought at a price; therefore glorify God in your body and in your spirit, which are God's.

1 CORINTHIANS 6:19–20

Everyone who competes for the prize is temperate in all things. Now they do it to obtain a perishable crown, but we for an imperishable crown. Therefore I run thus: not with uncertainty. Thus I fight: not as one who beats the air. But I discipline my body and bring it into subjection, lest, when I have preached to others, I myself should become disqualified.

1 CORINTHIANS 9:25–27

If we say that we have no sin, we deceive ourselves, and the truth is not in us. If we confess our sins, He is faithful and just to forgive us our sins and to cleanse us from all unrighteousness.

1 JOHN 1:8–9

Jesus answered them, "Most assuredly, I say to you, whoever commits sin is a slave of sin. And a slave does not abide in the house forever, but a son abides forever. Therefore if the Son makes you free, you shall be free indeed."

JOHN 8:34–36

Therefore, having these promises, beloved, let us cleanse ourselves from all filthiness of the flesh and spirit, perfecting holiness in the fear of God.

2 CORINTHIANS 7:1

Rejoice to the extent that you partake of Christ's sufferings, that when His glory is revealed, you may also be glad with exceeding joy.

1 PETER 4:13

For this reason we also . . . do not cease to pray for you . . . that you may walk worthy of the Lord, fully pleasing Him, being fruitful in every good work and increasing in the knowledge of God; strengthened with all might, according to His glorious power.

COLOSSIANS 1:9–11

ALIENATION FROM GOD

For I am persuaded that neither death nor life, nor angels nor principalities nor powers, nor things present nor things to come, nor height nor depth, nor any other created thing, shall be able to separate us from the love of God which is in Christ Jesus our Lord.

ROMANS 8:38–39

And you, who once were alienated and enemies in your mind by wicked works, yet now He has reconciled in the body of His flesh through death, to present you holy, and blameless, and above reproach in His sight.

COLOSSIANS 1:21–22

Seeing then that we have a great High Priest who has passed through the heavens, Jesus the Son of God, let us hold fast our confession. For we do not have a High Priest who cannot sympathize with our weaknesses, but was in all points tempted as we are, yet without sin. Let us therefore come boldly to the throne of grace, that we may obtain mercy and find grace to help in time of need.

HEBREWS 4:14–16

Give ear, O LORD, to my prayer;
And attend to the voice of my supplications.
In the day of my trouble I will call upon You,
For You will answer me.

PSALM 86:6–7

For I know the thoughts that I think toward you, says the Lord, thoughts of peace and not of evil, to give you a future and a hope. Then you will call upon Me and go and pray to Me, and I will listen to you. And you will seek Me and find Me, when you search for Me with all your heart.

JEREMIAH 29:11–13

For this reason I bow my knees to the Father of our Lord Jesus Christ, from whom the whole family in heaven and earth is named, that He would grant you, according to the riches of His glory, to be strengthened with might through His Spirit in the inner man, that Christ may dwell in your hearts through faith; that you, being rooted and grounded in love, may be able to comprehend with all the saints what is the width and length and depth and height—to know the love of Christ which passes knowledge; that you may be filled with all the fullness of God.

EPHESIANS 3:14–19

But you are a chosen generation, a royal priesthood, a holy nation, His own special people, that you may proclaim the praises of Him who called you out of darkness into His marvelous light; who once were not a people but are now the people of God, who had not obtained mercy but now have obtained mercy.

1 PETER 2:9–10

YOUR CONSCIENCE

But sanctify the Lord God in your hearts, and always be ready to give a defense to everyone who asks you a reason for the hope that is in you, with meekness and fear; having a good conscience, that when they defame you as evildoers, those who revile your good conduct in Christ may be ashamed.

1 PETER 3:15–16

My son, let them not depart from your eyes—
Keep sound wisdom and discretion;
So they will be life to your soul
And grace to your neck.
Then you will walk safely in your way,
And your foot will not stumble.
When you lie down, you will not be afraid;
Yes, you will lie down and your sleep will be sweet.

PROVERBS 3:21–24

How much more shall the blood of Christ, who through the eternal Spirit offered Himself without spot to God, cleanse your conscience from dead works to serve the living God?

HEBREWS 9:14

This being so, I myself always strive to have a conscience without offense toward God and men.

ACTS 24:16

Let us draw near with a true heart in full assurance of faith, having our hearts sprinkled from an evil conscience and our bodies washed with pure water.

HEBREWS 10:22

This charge I commit to you, son Timothy, according to the prophecies previously made concerning you, that by them you may wage the good warfare, having faith and a good conscience.

1 TIMOTHY 1:18–19

There is therefore now no condemnation to those who are in Christ Jesus, who do not walk according to the flesh, but according to the Spirit. For the law of the Spirit of life in Christ Jesus has made me free from the law of sin and death.

ROMANS 8:1–2

WHAT THE BIBLE HAS TO SAY ABOUT . . .
FOUL LANGUAGE

But fornication and all uncleanness or covetousness, let it not even be named among you, as is fitting for saints; neither filthiness, nor foolish talking, nor coarse jesting, which are not fitting, but rather giving of thanks.

EPHESIANS 5:3–4

Now you yourselves are to put off all these: anger, wrath, malice, blasphemy, filthy language out of your mouth.

COLOSSIANS 3:8

The words of a wise man's mouth are gracious,
But the lips of a fool shall swallow him up.

ECCLESIASTES 10:12

There is one who speaks like the piercings of a sword,
But the tongue of the wise promotes health.

PROVERBS 12:18

Whoever guards his mouth and tongue
Keeps his soul from troubles.

PROVERBS 21:23

Let your speech always be with grace, seasoned with salt, that you may know how you ought to answer each one.

COLOSSIANS 4:6

Let no corrupt word proceed out of your mouth, but what is good for necessary edification, that it may impart grace to the hearers.

EPHESIANS 4:29

Set a guard, O LORD, over my mouth;
Keep watch over the door of my lips.

PSALM 141:3

If anyone among you thinks he is religious, and does not bridle his tongue but deceives his own heart, this one's religion is useless.

JAMES 1:26

"But let your 'Yes' be 'Yes,' and your 'No,' 'No.' For whatever is more than these is from the evil one."

MATTHEW 5:37

WHAT THE BIBLE HAS TO SAY ABOUT . . .
HATE

Let all bitterness, wrath, anger, clamor, and evil speaking be put away from you, with all malice.

EPHESIANS 4:31

For you, brethren, have been called to liberty; only do not use liberty as an opportunity for the flesh, but through love serve one another. For all the law is fulfilled in one word, even in this: "You shall love your neighbor as yourself."

GALATIANS 5:13–14

Pursue peace with all people, and holiness, without which no one will see the LORD: looking carefully lest anyone fall short of the grace of God; lest any root of bitterness springing up cause trouble, and by this many become defiled.

HEBREWS 12:14–15

Do not be overcome by evil, but overcome evil with good.

ROMANS 12:21

For judgment is without mercy to the one who has shown no mercy. Mercy triumphs over judgment.

JAMES 2:13

And we have known and believed the love that God has for us. God is love, and he who abides in love abides in God, and God in him.

"A new commandment I give to you, that you love one another; as I have loved you, that you also love one another. By this all will know that you are My disciples, if you have love for one another."

JOHN 13:34–35

"Love your enemies, do good to those who hate you, bless those who curse you, and pray for those who spitefully use you."

LUKE 6:27–28

Let love be without hypocrisy. Abhor what is evil. Cling to what is good.

ROMANS 12:9

HOLINESS

Therefore be imitators of God as dear children.
And walk in love, as Christ also has loved us and given
Himself for us, an offering and a sacrifice to God for a
sweet-smelling aroma.

Ephesians 5:1–2

I beseech you therefore, brethren, by the mercies of
God, that you present your bodies a living sacrifice, holy,
acceptable to God, which is your reasonable service.

Romans 12:1

Come out from among them
And be separate, says the Lord.
Do not touch what is unclean,
And I will receive you.
I will be a Father to you,
And you shall be My sons and daughters,
Says the Lord Almighty.

2 Corinthians 6:17–18

If then you were raised with Christ, seek those things
which are above, where Christ is, sitting at the right
hand of God. Set your mind on things above, not on
things on the earth.

Colossians 3:1–2

Whatever you do in word or deed, do all in the name of the Lord Jesus, giving thanks to God the Father through Him.

COLOSSIANS 3:17

Work out your own salvation with fear and trembling; for it is God who works in you both to will and to do for His good pleasure. Do all things without complaining and disputing, that you may become blameless and harmless, children of God without fault in the midst of a crooked and perverse generation, among whom you shine as lights in the world.

PHILIPPIANS 2:12–15

Pursue peace with all people, and holiness, without which no one will see the Lord.

HEBREWS 12:14

As He who called you is holy, you also be holy in all your conduct, because it is written, "Be holy, for I am holy."

1 PETER 1:15–16

Finally then, brethren, we urge and exhort in the Lord Jesus that you should abound more and more, just as you received from us how you ought to walk and to please God; for you know what commandments we gave you through the Lord Jesus. . . . For God did not call us to uncleanness, but in holiness.

1 THESSALONIANS 4:1–2, 7

Whoever keeps His word, truly the love of God is perfected in him. By this we know that we are in Him. He who says he abides in Him ought himself also to walk just as He walked.

1 John 2:5–6

THE HOLY SPIRIT

"I will pray the Father, and He will give you another Helper, that He may abide with you forever—the Spirit of truth, whom the world cannot receive, because it neither sees Him nor knows Him; but you know Him, for He dwells with you and will be in you."

JOHN 14:16–17

"When He, the Spirit of truth, has come, He will guide you into all truth; for He will not speak on His own authority, but whatever He hears He will speak; and He will tell you things to come. He will glorify Me, for He will take of what is Mine and declare it to you."

JOHN 16:13–14

"But you shall receive power when the Holy Spirit has come upon you; and you shall be witnesses to Me in Jerusalem, and in all Judea and Samaria, and to the end of the earth."

ACTS 1:8

Walk as children of light (for the fruit of the Spirit is in all goodness, righteousness, and truth), finding out what is acceptable to the Lord.

EPHESIANS 5:8–10

If we live in the Spirit, let us also walk in the Spirit.

GALATIANS 5:25

For as many as are led by the Spirit of God, these are sons of God. For you did not receive the spirit of bondage again to fear, but you received the Spirit of adoption by whom we cry out, "Abba, Father." The Spirit Himself bears witness with our spirit that we are children of God.

ROMANS 8:14–16

But the fruit of the Spirit is love, joy, peace, longsuffering, kindness, goodness, faithfulness, gentleness, self-control. Against such there is no law.

GALATIANS 5:22–23

LEADING SOMEONE TO CHRIST

You, who once were alienated and enemies in your mind by wicked works, yet now He has reconciled in the body of His flesh through death, to present you holy, and blameless, and above reproach in His sight.

COLOSSIANS 1:21–22

For all have sinned and fall short of the glory of God, being justified freely by His grace through the redemption that is in Christ Jesus.

ROMANS 3:23–24

For the wages of sin is death, but the gift of God is eternal life in Christ Jesus our Lord.

ROMANS 6:23

"As Moses lifted up the serpent in the wilderness, even so must the Son of Man be lifted up, that whoever believes in Him should not perish but have eternal life. For God so loved the world that He gave His only begotten Son, that whoever believes in Him should not perish but have everlasting life."

JOHN 3:14–16

For by grace you have been saved through faith, and that not of yourselves; it is the gift of God, not of works, lest anyone should boast.

EPHESIANS 2:8–9

But when the kindness and the love of God our Savior toward man appeared, not by works of righteousness which we have done, but according to His mercy He saved us, through the washing of regeneration and renewing of the Holy Spirit, whom He poured out on us abundantly through Jesus Christ our Savior, that having been justified by His grace we should become heirs according to the hope of eternal life.

TITUS 3:4–7

Jesus said to him, "I am the way, the truth, and the life. No one comes to the Father except through Me."

JOHN 14:6

If you confess with your mouth the Lord Jesus and believe in your heart that God has raised Him from the dead, you will be saved. For with the heart one believes unto righteousness, and with the mouth confession is made unto salvation.

ROMANS 10:9–10

LOVE OF GOD

God demonstrates His own love toward us, in that while we were still sinners, Christ died for us.

ROMANS 5:8

"The Father Himself loves you, because you have loved Me, and have believed that I came forth from God."

JOHN 16:27

I am persuaded that neither death nor life, nor angels nor principalities nor powers, nor things present nor things to come, nor height nor depth, nor any other created thing, shall be able to separate us from the love of God which is in Christ Jesus our Lord.

ROMANS 8:38–39

God, who is rich in mercy, because of His great love with which He loved us, even when we were dead in trespasses, made us alive together with Christ (by grace you have been saved).

EPHESIANS 2:4–5

That Christ may dwell in your hearts through faith; that you, being rooted and grounded in love, may be able to comprehend with all the saints what is the width and length and depth and height—to know the love of Christ which passes knowledge; that you may be filled with all the fullness of God.

EPHESIANS 3:17–19

Behold what manner of love the Father has bestowed on us, that we should be called children of God! Therefore the world does not know us, because it did not know Him.

1 JOHN 3:1

"Greater love has no one than this, than to lay down one's life for his friends."

JOHN 15:13

In this is love, not that we loved God, but that He loved us and sent His Son to be the propitiation for our sins.

1 JOHN 4:10

"For God so loved the world that He gave His only begotten Son, that whoever believes in Him should not perish but have everlasting life."

JOHN 3:16

Jesus said to him, "'You shall love the LORD your God with all your heart, with all your soul, and with all your mind.' This is the first and great commandment. And the second is like it: 'You shall love your neighbor as yourself.'"

MATTHEW 22:37–39

Jesus answered and said to him, "If anyone loves Me, he will keep My word; and My Father will love him, and We will come to him and make Our home with him."

JOHN 14:23–24

LOVE OF OTHERS

And above all things have fervent love for one another, for "love will cover a multitude of sins."

1 PETER 4:8

By this we know love, because He laid down His life for us. And we also ought to lay down our lives for the brethren.

1 JOHN 3:16

Finally, all of you be of one mind, having compassion for one another; love as brothers, be tenderhearted, be courteous.

1 PETER 3:8

Let love be without hypocrisy. Abhor what is evil. Cling to what is good. Be kindly affectionate to one another with brotherly love, in honor giving preference to one another.

ROMANS 12:9–10

Since you have purified your souls in obeying the truth through the Spirit in sincere love of the brethren, love one another fervently with a pure heart.

1 PETER 1:22

Therefore, as we have opportunity, let us do good to all, especially to those who are of the household of faith.

GALATIANS 6:10

"If I then, your Lord and Teacher, have washed your feet, you also ought to wash one another's feet. For I have given you an example, that you should do as I have done to you."

JOHN 13:14–15

But above all these things put on love, which is the bond of perfection.

COLOSSIANS 3:14

Love suffers long and is kind; love does not envy; love does not parade itself, is not puffed up.

1 CORINTHIANS 13:4

May the Lord make you increase and abound in love to one another and to all.

1 THESSALONIANS 3:12

MARRIAGE

And the LORD God said, "It is not good that man should be alone; I will make him a helper comparable to him."

GENESIS 2:18

Two are better than one,
Because they have a good reward for their labor.
For if they fall, one will lift up his companion.
But woe to him who is alone when he falls,
For he has no one to help him up.
Again, if two lie down together, they will keep warm;
But how can one be warm alone?
Though one may be overpowered by another,
   two can withstand him.
And a threefold cord is not quickly broken.

ECCLESIASTES 4:9–12

Love suffers long and is kind; love does not envy; love does not parade itself, is not puffed up; does not behave rudely, does not seek its own, is not provoked, thinks no evil; does not rejoice in iniquity, but rejoices in the truth; bears all things, believes all things, hopes all things, endures all things. Love never fails.

1 CORINTHIANS 13:4–8

He who finds a wife finds a good thing,
And obtains favor from the LORD.

PROVERBS 18:22

And He answered and said to them, "Have you not read that He who made them at the beginning 'made them male and female,' and said, 'For this reason a man shall leave his father and mother and be joined to his wife, and the two shall become one flesh'? So then, they are no longer two but one flesh. Therefore what God has joined together, let not man separate."

MATTHEW 19:4–6

Houses and riches are an inheritance from fathers,
But a prudent wife is from the LORD.

PROVERBS 19:14

Let your fountain be blessed,
And rejoice with the wife of your youth.

PROVERBS 5:18

And be kind to one another, tenderhearted, forgiving one another, even as God in Christ forgave you.

EPHESIANS 4:32

Or do you not know that your body is the temple of the Holy Spirit who is in you, whom you have from God, and you are not your own? For you were bought at a price; therefore glorify God in your body and in your spirit, which are God's.

1 CORINTHIANS 6:19–20

Wives, submit to your own husbands, as to the Lord. For the husband is head of the wife, as also Christ is head of the church; and He is the Savior of the body. Therefore, just as the church is subject to Christ, so let the wives be to their own husbands in everything.

Husbands, love your wives, just as Christ also loved the church and gave Himself for her, that He might sanctify and cleanse her with the washing of water by the word, that He might present her to Himself a glorious church, not having spot or wrinkle or any such thing, but that she should be holy and without blemish. So husbands ought to love their own wives as their own bodies; he who loves his wife loves himself. For no one ever hated his own flesh, but nourishes and cherishes it, just as the Lord does the church. For we are members of His body, of His flesh and of His bones.

"For this reason a man shall leave his father and mother and be joined to his wife, and the two shall become one flesh." This is a great mystery, but I speak concerning Christ and the church. Nevertheless let each one of you in particular so love his own wife as himself, and let the wife see that she respects her husband.

EPHESIANS 5:22–33

WHAT THE BIBLE HAS TO SAY ABOUT . . .
MONEY

"No servant can serve two masters; for either he will hate the one and love the other, or else he will be loyal to the one and despise the other. You cannot serve God and mammon."

LUKE 16:13

For the love of money is a root of all kinds of evil, for which some have strayed from the faith in their greediness, and pierced themselves through with many sorrows.

1 TIMOTHY 6:10

"Bring all the tithes into the storehouse,
That there may be food in My house,
And try Me now in this," Says the LORD of hosts,
"If I will not open for you the windows of heaven
And pour out for you such blessing
That there will not be room enough to receive it."

MALACHI 3:10

Give generously to the poor, not grudgingly, for the LORD your God will bless you in everything you do.

DEUTERONOMY 15:10 NLT

The generous soul will be made rich,
And he who waters will also be watered himself.

PROVERBS 11:25

So let each one give as he purposes in his heart, not grudgingly or of necessity; for God loves a cheerful giver.

2 CORINTHIANS 9:7

Not that I speak in regard to need, for I have learned in whatever state I am, to be content: I know how to be abased, and I know how to abound. Everywhere and in all things I have learned both to be full and to be hungry, both to abound and to suffer need.

PHILIPPIANS 4:11–12

Why do you spend money for what is not bread,
And your wages for what does not satisfy?
Listen carefully to Me, and eat what is good,
And let your soul delight itself in abundance.

ISAIAH 55:2

OBEDIENCE

Let every soul be subject to the governing authorities. For there is no authority except from God, and the authorities that exist are appointed by God.

ROMANS 13:1

Children, obey your parents in all things, for this is well pleasing to the Lord.

COLOSSIANS 3:20

Remind them to be subject to rulers and authorities, to obey, to be ready for every good work, to speak evil of no one, to be peaceable, gentle, showing all humility to all men.

TITUS 3:1–2

Submit yourselves to every ordinance of man for the Lord's sake, whether to the king as supreme, or to governors, as to those who are sent by him for the punishment of evildoers and for the praise of those who do good.

1 PETER 2:13–14

Now therefore, if you will indeed obey My voice and keep My covenant, then you shall be a special treasure to Me above all people; for all the earth is Mine.

EXODUS 19:5

Meditate on these things; give yourself entirely to them, that your progress may be evident to all.

1 TIMOTHY 4:15

This is what I commanded them, saying, "Obey My voice, and I will be your God, and you shall be My people. And walk in all the ways that I have commanded you, that it may be well with you." Yet they did not obey or incline their ear, but followed the counsels and the dictates of their evil hearts, and went backward and not forward.

JEREMIAH 7:23–24

OVERCOMING EVIL

Repay no one evil for evil. Have regard for good things in the sight of all men. If it is possible, as much as depends on you, live peaceably with all men. Beloved, do not avenge yourselves, but rather give place to wrath; for it is written, "Vengeance is Mine, I will repay," says the Lord. Therefore

"If your enemy is hungry, feed him;
If he is thirsty, give him a drink;
For in so doing you will heap coals of fire on his head."

ROMANS 12:17–20

All of you be of one mind, having compassion for one another; love as brothers, be tenderhearted, be courteous; not returning evil for evil or reviling for reviling, but on the contrary blessing, knowing that you were called to this, that you may inherit a blessing.

1 PETER 3:8–9

You are of God, little children, and have overcome them, because He who is in you is greater than he who is in the world.

1 JOHN 4:4

Beloved, do not imitate what is evil, but what is good. He who does good is of God, but he who does evil has not seen God.

3 JOHN V. 11

Do not say, "I will recompense evil";
Wait for the LORD, and He will save you.

PROVERBS 20:22

Bless those who persecute you; bless and do not curse.

ROMANS 12:14

Yea, though I walk through the valley of the shadow
 of death,
I will fear no evil;
For You are with me;
Your rod and Your staff, they comfort me.

PSALM 23:4

Depart from evil, and do good;
And dwell forevermore.
For the LORD loves justice,
And does not forsake His saints.

PSALM 37:27–28

You who love the LORD, hate evil!
He preserves the souls of His saints;
He delivers them out of the hand of the wicked.

PSALM 97:10

Let all bitterness, wrath, anger, clamor, and evil
speaking be put away from you, with all malice. And
be kind to one another, tenderhearted, forgiving one
another, even as God in Christ forgave you.

EPHESIANS 4:31–32

Lord, who may abide in Your tabernacle?
Who may dwell in Your holy hill?
He who walks uprightly,
And works righteousness,
And speaks the truth in his heart.

Psalm 15:1–2

Keep you tongue from evil,
And your lips from speaking deceit.
Depart from evil and do good;
Seek peace and pursue it.
The eyes of the Lord are on the righteous,
And His ears are open to their cry.

Psalm 34:13–15

PATIENCE AND PERSEVERANCE

Rest in the LORD, and wait patiently for Him;
Do not fret because of him who prospers in his way,
Because of the man who brings wicked schemes to pass.

PSALM 37:7

I waited patiently for the LORD;
And He inclined to me,
And heard my cry.

PSALM 40:1

Therefore we do not lose heart. Even though our outward man is perishing, yet the inward man is being renewed day by day. For our light affliction, which is but for a moment, is working for us a far more exceeding and eternal weight of glory, while we do not look at the things which are seen, but at the things which are not seen. For the things which are seen are temporary, but the things which are not seen are eternal.

2 CORINTHIANS 4:16–18

Be patient, brethren, until the coming of the Lord. See how the farmer waits for the precious fruit of the earth, waiting patiently for it until it receives the early and latter rain. You also be patient. Establish your hearts, for the coming of the Lord is at hand.

JAMES 5:7–8

But also for this very reason, giving all diligence, add to your faith virtue, to virtue knowledge, to knowledge self-control, to self-control perseverance, to perseverance godliness, to godliness brotherly kindness, and to brotherly kindness love. For if these things are yours and abound, you will be neither barren nor unfruitful in the knowledge of our Lord Jesus Christ.

2 PETER 1:5–8

Count it all joy when you fall into various trials, knowing that the testing of your faith produces patience. But let patience have its perfect work, that you may be perfect and complete, lacking nothing.

JAMES 1:2–4

The LORD is good to those who wait for Him,
To the soul who seeks Him.
It is good that one should hope and wait quietly
For the salvation of the LORD.
It is good for a man to bear
The yoke in his youth.

LAMENTATIONS 3:25–27

May the God of patience and comfort grant you to be like-minded toward one another, according to Christ Jesus, that you may with one mind and one mouth glorify the God and Father of our Lord Jesus Christ.

ROMANS 15:5–6

But none of these things move me; nor do I count my life dear to myself, so that I may finish my race with joy, and the ministry which I received from the Lord Jesus, to testify to the gospel of the grace of God.

ACTS 20:24

The LORD is my rock and my fortress and my deliverer;
My God, my strength, in whom I will trust;
My shield and the horn of my salvation, my
   stronghold.

PSALM 18:2

"Because you have kept My command to perservere, I also will keep you from the hour of trial which shall come upon the whole world, to test those who dwell on earth."

REVELATION 3:10

PRAISE

Because Your lovingkindness is better than life,
My lips shall praise You.
Thus I will bless You while I live;
I will lift up my hands in Your name.

PSALM 63:3–4

For the LORD is great and greatly to be praised;
He is to be feared above all gods.

PSALM 96:4

Enter into His gates with thanksgiving,
And into His courts with praise.
Be thankful to Him, and bless His name.

PSALM 100:4

Even so we speak, not as pleasing men, but God who
tests our hearts.

1 THESSALONIANS 2:4

"Let your light so shine before men, that they may see
your good works and glorify your Father in heaven."

MATTHEW 5:16

This people I have formed for Myself;
They shall declare My praise.

ISAIAH 43:21

By Him let us continually offer the sacrifice of praise to
God, that is, the fruit of our lips, giving thanks to His name.

HEBREWS 13:15

You are a chosen generation, a royal priesthood,
a holy nation, His own special people, that you may
proclaim the praises of Him who called you out of
darkness into His marvelous light.

1 PETER 2:9

Therefore judge nothing before the time, until the
LORD comes, who will bring to light the hidden things
of darkness and reveal the counsels of the hearts. Then
each one's praise will come from God.

1 CORINTHIANS 4:5

Praise the LORD!
For it is good to sing praises to our God;
For it is pleasant, and praise is beautiful.

PSALM 147:1

While I live I will praise the LORD;
I will sing praises to my God while I have my being. . . .
Happy is he who has the God of Jacob for his help,
Whose hope is in the LORD his God.

PSALM 146:2, 5

Praise the LORD!
Praise God in His sanctuary;
Praise Him in His mighty firmament!
Praise Him for His mighty acts;
Praise Him according to His excellent greatness!
Praise Him with the sound of the trumpet;
Praise Him with the lute and harp!
Praise Him with the timbrel and dance;
Praise Him with stringed instruments and flutes!
Praise Him with loud cymbals;
Praise Him with clashing cymbals!
Let everything that has breath praise the LORD.
Praise the LORD!

PSALM 150:1–6

PRIDE

When pride comes, then comes shame;
But with the humble is wisdom.

PROVERBS 11:2

The fear of the LORD is the instruction of wisdom,
And before honor is humility.

PROVERBS 15:33

A man's pride will bring him low,
But the humble in spirit will retain honor.

PROVERBS 29:23

Thus says the LORD:
"Let not the wise man glory in his wisdom,
Let not the mighty man glory in his might,
Nor let the rich man glory in his riches;
But let him who glories glory in this,
That he understands and knows Me,
That I am the LORD, exercising lovingkindness,
    judgment, and righteousness in the earth.
For in these I delight," says the LORD.

JEREMIAH 9:23–24

"Whoever exalts himself will be humbled, and he who
humbles himself will be exalted."

LUKE 14:11

If anyone else thinks he may have confidence in the flesh, I more so. . . . But what things were gain to me, these I have counted loss for Christ. Yet indeed I also count all things loss for the excellence of the knowledge of Christ Jesus my Lord, for whom I have suffered the loss of all things, and count them as rubbish, that I may gain Christ.

PHILIPPIANS 3:4, 7–8

"Whoever desires to become great among you, let him be your servant. And whoever desires to be first among you, let him be your slave."

MATTHEW 20:26–27

For I say, through the grace given to me, to everyone who is among you, not to think of himself more highly than he ought to think, but to think soberly, as God has dealt to each one a measure of faith.

ROMANS 12:3

"For all those things My hand has made,
And all those things exist,"
Says the LORD.
"But on this one will I look:
On him who is poor and of a contrite spirit,
And who trembles at My word."

ISAIAH 66:2

By pride comes nothing but strife,
But with the well-advised is wisdom.

PROVERBS 13:10

Let nothing be done through selfish ambition or conceit, but in lowliness of mind let each esteem others better than himself. Let each of you look out not only for his own interests, but also for the interests of others.

PHILIPPIANS 2:3–4

Likewise you younger people, submit yourselves to your elders. Yes, all of you be submissive to one another, and be clothed with humility, for
"God resists the proud,
But gives grace to the humble."

1 PETER 5:5

WHAT THE BIBLE HAS TO SAY ABOUT . . .
PURITY

Finally, brethren, whatever things are true, whatever things are noble, whatever things are just, whatever things are pure, whatever things are lovely, whatever things are of good report, if there is any virtue and if there is anything praiseworthy—meditate on these things. The things which you learned and received and heard and saw in me, these do, and the God of peace will be with you.

PHILIPPIANS 4:8–9

I say then: Walk in the Spirit, and you shall not fulfill the lust of the flesh.

GALATIANS 5:16

No temptation has overtaken you except such as is common to man; but God is faithful, who will not allow you to be tempted beyond what you are able, but with the temptation will also make the way of escape, that you may be able to bear it.

1 CORINTHIANS 10:13

The grace of God that brings salvation has appeared to all men, teaching us that, denying ungodliness and worldly lusts, we should live soberly, righteously, and godly in the present age.

TITUS 2:11–12

Therefore put to death your members which are on the earth: fornication, uncleanness, passion, evil desire, and covetousness, which is idolatry.

COLOSSIANS 3:5

For you were bought at a price; therefore glorify God in your body and in your spirit, which are God's.

1 CORINTHIANS 6:20

And do not present your members as instruments of unrighteousness to sin, but present yourselves to God as being alive from the dead, and your members as instruments of righteousness to God.

ROMANS 6:13

For the law of the Spirit of life in Christ Jesus has made me free from the law of sin and death.

ROMANS 8:2

WHAT THE BIBLE HAS TO SAY ABOUT . . .
SATAN

Be strong in the Lord and in the power of His might. Put on the whole armor of God, that you may be able to stand against the wiles of the devil. For we do not wrestle against flesh and blood, but against principalities, against powers, against the rulers of the darkness of this age, against spiritual hosts of wickedness in the heavenly places. Therefore take up the whole armor of God, that you may be able to withstand in the evil day, and having done all, to stand.

EPHESIANS 6:10–13

Submit to God. Resist the devil and he will flee from you. Draw near to God and He will draw near to you.

JAMES 4:7–8

Be sober, be vigilant; because your adversary the devil walks about like a roaring lion, seeking whom he may devour. Resist him, steadfast in the faith, knowing that the same sufferings are experienced by your brotherhood in the world.

1 PETER 5:8–9

The night is far spent, the day is at hand. Therefore let us cast off the works of darkness, and let us put on the armor of light.

ROMANS 13:12

"In the world you will have tribulation; but be of good cheer, I have overcome the world."

John 16:33

If then you were raised with Christ, seek those things which are above, where Christ is, sitting at the right hand of God. Set your mind on things above, not on things on the earth. For you died, and your life is hidden with Christ in God.

Colossians 3:1–3

Though we walk in the flesh, we do not war according to the flesh. For the weapons of our warfare are not carnal but mighty in God for pulling down strongholds, casting down arguments and every high thing that exalts itself against the knowledge of God, bringing every thought into captivity to the obedience of Christ.

2 Corinthians 10:3–5

WHAT THE BIBLE HAS TO SAY ABOUT . . .
SELF-CENTEREDNESS

Let nothing be done through selfish ambition or conceit, but in lowliness of mind let each esteem others better than himself. Let each of you look out not only for his own interests, but also for the interests of others.

PHILIPPIANS 2:3–4

Then He said to them all, "If anyone desires to come after Me, let him deny himself, and take up his cross daily, and follow Me. For whoever desires to save his life will lose it, but whoever loses his life for My sake will save it. For what profit is it to a man if he gains the whole world, and is himself destroyed or lost?"

LUKE 9:23–25

"By this all will know that you are My disciples, if you have love for one another."

JOHN 13:35

Be kindly affectionate to one another with brotherly love, in honor giving preference to one another.

ROMANS 12:10

Let each of us please his neighbor for his good, leading to edification. For even Christ did not please Himself; but as it is written, "The reproaches of those who reproached You fell on Me."

ROMANS 15:2–3

Bear one another's burdens, and so fulfill the law of Christ.

GALATIANS 6:2

"Whoever desires to become great among you, let him be your servant. And whoever desires to be first among you, let him be your slave—just as the Son of Man did not come to be served, but to serve, and to give His life a ransom for many."

MATTHEW 20:26–28

Let no one seek his own, but each one the other's well-being.

1 CORINTHIANS 10:24

WHAT THE BIBLE HAS TO SAY ABOUT . . .
SELF-CONTROL

For this very reason, giving all diligence, add to your faith virtue, to virtue knowledge, to knowledge self-control, to self-control perseverance, to perseverance godliness.

2 PETER 1:5–6

Be renewed in the spirit of your mind, and that you put on the new man which was created according to God, in true righteousness and holiness.

EPHESIANS 4:23–24

A fool vents all his feelings,
But a wise man holds them back.

PROVERBS 29:11

Everyone who competes for the prize is temperate in all things. Now they do it to obtain a perishable crown, but we for an imperishable crown. Therefore I run thus: not with uncertainty. Thus I fight: not as one who beats the air. But I discipline my body and bring it into subjection, lest, when I have preached to others, I myself should become disqualified.

1 CORINTHIANS 9:25–27

Therefore let us not sleep, as others do, but let us watch and be sober. For those who sleep, sleep at night, and those who get drunk are drunk at night. But let us who are of the day be sober, putting on the breastplate of faith and love, and as a helmet the hope of salvation.

1 THESSALONIANS 5:6–8

The fruit of the Spirit is love, joy, peace, longsuffering, kindness, goodness, faithfulness, gentleness, self-control. Against such there is no law. And those who are Christ's have crucified the flesh with its passions and desires.

GALATIANS 5:22–24

SEX LIFE

"Blessed are the pure in heart,
For they shall see God."

MATTHEW 5:8

Let your fountain be blessed,
And rejoice with the wife of your youth.

PROVERBS 5:18

Do you not know that your bodies are members of Christ? Shall I then take the members of Christ and make them members of a harlot? Certainly not! Or do you not know that he who is joined to a harlot is one body with her? For "the two," He says, "shall become one flesh." But he who is joined to the Lord is one spirit with Him.

Flee sexual immorality. Every sin that a man does is outside the body, but he who commits sexual immorality sins against his own body. Or do you not know that your body is the temple of the Holy Spirit who is in you, whom you have from God, and you are not your own? For you were bought at a price; therefore glorify God in your body and in your spirit, which are God's.

1 CORINTHIANS 6:15–20

But if we walk in the light as He is in the light, we have fellowship with one another, and the blood of Jesus Christ His Son cleanses us from all sin.

1 JOHN 1:7

This is the will of God, your sanctification: that you should abstain from sexual immorality; that each of you should know how to possess his own vessel in sanctification and honor, not in passion of lust, like the Gentiles who do not know God.

1 Thessalonians 4:3–5

Flee also youthful lusts; but pursue righteousness, faith, love, peace with those who call on the Lord out of a pure heart.

2 Timothy 2:22

Marriage is honorable among all, and the bed undefiled; but fornicators and adulterers God will judge.

Hebrews 13:4

Do not love the world or the things in the world. If anyone loves the world, the love of the Father is not in him. For all that is in the world—the lust of the flesh, the lust of the eyes, and the pride of life—is not of the Father but is of the world.

1 John 2:15–16

TEMPTATION

No temptation has overtaken you except such as is common to man; but God is faithful, who will not allow you to be tempted beyond what you are able, but with the temptation will also make the way of escape, that you may be able to bear it.

1 Corinthians 10:13

For in that He Himself has suffered, being tempted, He is able to aid those who are tempted.

Hebrews 2:18

Be strong in the Lord and in the power of His might. Put on the whole armor of God, that you may be able to stand against the wiles of the devil. For we do not wrestle against flesh and blood, but against principalities, against powers, against the rulers of the darkness of this age, against spiritual hosts of wickedness in the heavenly places.

Ephesians 6:10–12

For we do not have a High Priest who cannot sympathize with our weaknesses, but was in all points tempted as we are, yet without sin. Let us therefore come boldly to the throne of grace, that we may obtain mercy and find grace to help in time of need.

Hebrews 4:15–16

Blessed is the man who endures temptation; for when he has been approved, he will receive the crown of life which the Lord has promised to those who love Him.

JAMES 1:12

"Watch and pray, lest you enter into temptation. The spirit indeed is willing, but the flesh is weak."

MATTHEW 26:41

Search me, O God, and know my heart;
Try me, and know my anxieties;
And see if there is any wicked way in me,
And lead me in the way everlasting.

PSALM 139:23–24

"In this manner, therefore, pray: . . .
And do not lead us into temptation,
But deliver us from the evil one.
For Yours is the kingdom and the power and the
    glory forever. Amen."

MATTHEW 6:9, 13

Your word I have hidden in my heart,
That I might not sin against You.

PSALM 119:11

THANKFULNESS

Make a joyful shout to the LORD, all you lands!
Serve the LORD with gladness;
Come before His presence with singing.
Know that the LORD, He is God;
It is He who has made us, and not we ourselves;
We are His people and the sheep of His pasture.
Enter into His gates with thanksgiving,
And into His courts with praise.
Be thankful to Him, and bless His name.
For the LORD is good;
His mercy is everlasting,
And His truth endures to all generations.

PSALM 100:1–5

In everything give thanks; for this is the will of God in Christ Jesus for you.

1 THESSALONIANS 5:18

Offer to God thanksgiving,
And pay your vows to the Most High.

PSALM 50:14

Oh, give thanks to the LORD!
Call upon His name;
Make known His deeds among the peoples!

PSALM 105:1

Speaking to one another in psalms and hymns and spiritual songs, singing and making melody in your heart to the Lord, giving thanks always for all things to God the Father in the name of our Lord Jesus Christ.

EPHESIANS 5:19–20

Let the peace of God rule in your hearts, to which also you were called in one body; and be thankful.

COLOSSIANS 3:15

By Him let us continually offer the sacrifice of praise to God, that is, the fruit of our lips, giving thanks to His name.

HEBREWS 13:15

He who observes the day, observes it to the Lord. . . . He who eats, eats to the Lord for he gives God thanks.

ROMANS 14:6

Now thanks be to God who always leads us in triumph in Christ, and through us diffuses the fragrance of its knowledge in every place.

2 CORINTHIANS 2:14

WHAT THE BIBLE HAS TO SAY ABOUT . . .
TRUST

Trust in the LORD with all your heart,
And lean not on your own understanding;
In all your ways acknowledge Him,
And He shall direct your paths.

PROVERBS 3:5–6

O LORD of hosts,
Blessed is the man who trusts in You!

PSALM 84:12

Do not put your trust in princes,
Nor in a son of man, in whom there is no help. . . .
Happy is he who has the God of Jacob for his help,
Whose hope is in the Lord his God.

PSALM 146:3, 5

Trust in the LORD, and do good;
Dwell in the land, and feed on His faithfulness.

PSALM 37:3

You will keep him in perfect peace,
Whose mind is stayed on You,
Because he trusts in You.
Trust in the LORD forever,
For in YAH, the LORD, is everlasting strength.

ISAIAH 26:3–4

He will not be afraid of evil tidings;
His heart is steadfast, trusting in the LORD.

PSALM 112:7

Let Your mercies come also to me, O LORD—
Your salvation according to Your word.
So shall I have an answer for him who reproaches me,
For I trust in Your word.

PSALM 119:41–42

The LORD is good,
A stronghold in the day of trouble;
And He knows those who trust in Him.

NAHUM 1:7

"Let not your heart be troubled; you believe in God,
believe also in Me."

JOHN 14:1

TRUTH

Then Jesus said to those Jews who believed Him, "If you abide in My word, you are My disciples indeed. And you shall know the truth, and the truth shall make you free."

JOHN 8:31–32

Jesus said to him, "I am the way, the truth, and the life. No one comes to the Father except through Me."

JOHN 14:6

"When He, the Spirit of truth, has come, He will guide you into all truth; for He will not speak on His own authority, but whatever He hears He will speak; and He will tell you things to come."

JOHN 16:13

Be diligent to present yourself approved to God, a worker who does not need to be ashamed, rightly dividing the word of truth.

2 TIMOTHY 2:15

Your righteousness is an everlasting righteousness,
And Your law is truth. . . .
The entirety of Your word is truth,
And every one of Your righteous judgments endures
    forever.

PSALM 119:142, 160

In Him you also trusted, after you heard the word of truth, the gospel of your salvation; in whom also, having believed, you were sealed with the Holy Spirit of promise.

EPHESIANS 1:13

Oh, how I love Your law!
It is my meditation all the day.
You, through Your commandments, make me wiser
   than my enemies;
For they are ever with me.
I have more understanding than all my teachers,
For Your testimonies are my meditation.
I understand more than the ancients,
Because I keep Your precepts.

PSALM 119:97–100

UNPLANNED PREGNANCY

For You formed my inward parts;
You covered me in my mother's womb.
I will praise You, for I am fearfully and wonderfully made;
Marvelous are Your works,
And that my soul knows very well.
My frame was not hidden from You,
When I was made in secret,
And skillfully wrought in the lowest parts of the earth.
Your eyes saw my substance, being yet unformed.
And in Your book they all were written,
The days fashioned for me,
When as yet there were none of them.

PSALM 139:13–16

The LORD is merciful and gracious,
Slow to anger, and abounding in mercy.
He will not always strive with us,
Nor will He keep His anger forever.
He has not dealt with us according to our sins,
Nor punished us according to our iniquities.
For as the heavens are high above the earth,
So great is His mercy toward those who fear Him;
As far as the east is from the west,
So far has He removed our transgressions from us.

PSALM 103:8–12

And we know that all things work together for good
to those who love God, to those who are the called
according to His purpose.

ROMANS 8:28

Behold, children are a heritage from the LORD,
The fruit of the womb is a reward.

PSALM 127:3

Those who wait on the LORD
Shall renew their strength;
They shall mount up with wings like eagles,
They shall run and not be weary,
They shall walk and not faint.

ISAIAH 40:31

Before I formed you in the womb I knew you;
Before you were born I sanctified you;
I ordained you a prophet to the nations.

JEREMIAH 1:5

Why are you cast down, O my soul?
And why are you disquieted within me?
Hope in God;
For I shall yet praise Him,
The help of my countenance and my God.

PSALM 42:11

UNSELFISHNESS

Let nothing be done through selfish ambition or conceit, but in lowliness of mind let each esteem others better than himself. Let each of you look out not only for his own interests, but also for the interests of others.

PHILIPPIANS 2:3–4

Bear one another's burdens, and so fulfill the law of Christ.

GALATIANS 6:2

He who has pity on the poor lends to the LORD,
And He will pay back what he has given.

PROVERBS 19:17

Rejoice with those who rejoice, and weep with those who weep. Be of the same mind toward one another.

ROMANS 12:15–16

Be kindly affectionate to one another with brotherly love, in honor giving preference to one another . . . distributing to the needs of the saints, given to hospitality.

ROMANS 12:10, 13

If you really fulfill the royal law according to the Scripture, "You shall love your neighbor as yourself," you do well.

JAMES 2:8

Therefore be imitators of God as dear children. And walk in love, as Christ also has loved us and given Himself for us, an offering and a sacrifice to God for a sweet-smelling aroma.

EPHESIANS 5:1–2

Give generously to the poor, not grudgingly, for the LORD your God will bless you in everything you do.

DEUTERONOMY 15:10 NLT

The generous soul will be made rich, And he who waters will also be watered himself.

PROVERBS 11:25

WORLDLINESS

If then you were raised with Christ, seek those things which are above, where Christ is, sitting at the right hand of God. Set your mind on things above, not on things on the earth.

COLOSSIANS 3:1–2

Do not be conformed to this world, but be transformed by the renewing of your mind, that you may prove what is that good and acceptable and perfect will of God.

ROMANS 12:2

For though we walk in the flesh, we do not war according to the flesh. For the weapons of our warfare are not carnal but mighty in God for pulling down strongholds.

2 CORINTHIANS 10:3–4

For the grace of God that brings salvation has appeared to all men, teaching us that, denying ungodliness and worldly lusts, we should live soberly, righteously, and godly in the present age, looking for the blessed hope and glorious appearing of our great God and Savior Jesus Christ, who gave Himself for us, that He might redeem us from every lawless deed and purify for Himself His own special people, zealous for good works.

TITUS 2:11–14

For our citizenship is in heaven, from which we also eagerly wait for the Savior, the Lord Jesus Christ, who will transform our lowly body that it may be conformed to His glorious body, according to the working by which He is able even to subdue all things to Himself. Therefore, my beloved and longed-for brethren, my joy and crown, so stand fast in the Lord, beloved.

PHILIPPIANS 3:20–4:1

Beloved, I beg you as sojourners and pilgrims, abstain from fleshly lusts which war against the soul.

1 PETER 2:11

God has chosen the foolish things of the world to put to shame the wise, and God has chosen the weak things of the world to put to shame the things which are mighty.

1 CORINTHIANS 1:27

Behold what manner of love the Father has bestowed on us, that we should be called children of God! Therefore the world does not know us, because it did not know Him.

1 JOHN 3:1

WHAT THE BIBLE HAS TO SAY ABOUT . . .
WITNESSING

He said to them, "Go into all the world and preach the gospel to every creature."

MARK 16:15

Then He said to them, "Thus it is written, and thus it was necessary for the Christ to suffer and to rise from the dead the third day, and that repentance and remission of sins should be preached in His name to all nations, beginning at Jerusalem."

LUKE 24:46–47

"You shall receive power when the Holy Spirit has come upon you; and you shall be witnesses to Me in Jerusalem, and in all Judea and Samaria, and to the end of the earth."

ACTS 1:8

Jesus came and spoke to them, saying, "All authority has been given to Me in heaven and on earth. Go therefore and make disciples of all the nations, baptizing them in the name of the Father and of the Son and of the Holy Spirit, teaching them to observe all things that I have commanded you; and lo, I am with you always, even to the end of the age." Amen.

MATTHEW 28:18–20

"You are My witnesses," says the LORD,
"And My servant whom I have chosen,
That you may know and believe Me,
And understand that I am He.
Before Me there was no God formed,
Nor shall there be after Me."

ISAIAH 43:10

For we do not preach ourselves, but Christ Jesus the Lord, and ourselves your bondservants for Jesus' sake. For it is the God who commanded light to shine out of darkness, who has shone in our hearts to give the light of the knowledge of the glory of God in the face of Jesus Christ.

2 CORINTHIANS 4:5–6

WORK

And whatever you do in word or deed, do all in the name of the Lord Jesus, giving thanks to God the Father through Him.

COLOSSIANS 3:17

Let him who stole steal no longer, but rather let him labor, working with his hands what is good, that he may have something to give to him who has need.

EPHESIANS 4:28

That you also aspire to lead a quiet life, to mind your own business, and to work with your own hands, as we commanded you, that you may walk properly toward those who are outside, and that you may lack nothing.

1 THESSALONIANS 4:11–12

And let the beauty of the LORD our God be upon us,
And establish the work of our hands for us;
Yes, establish the work of our hands.

PSALM 90:17

Now those who are such we command and exhort through our Lord Jesus Christ that they work in quietness and eat their own bread. But as for you, brethren, do not grow weary in doing good.

2 THESSALONIANS 3:12–13

Whether you eat or drink, or whatever you do, do all to the glory of God.

1 Corinthians 10:31

Let our people also learn to maintain good works, to meet urgent needs, that they may not be unfruitful.

Titus 3:14

He who looks into the perfect law of liberty and continues in it, and is not a forgetful hearer but a doer of the work, this one will be blessed in what he does.

James 1:25

YOUTH

Let no one despise your youth, but be an example to the believers in word, in conduct, in love, in spirit, in faith, in purity.

1 TIMOTHY 4:12

O God, You have taught me from my youth;
And to this day I declare Your wondrous works.

PSALM 71:17

Hear the instruction of your father,
And do not forsake the law of your mother;
For they will be a graceful ornament on your head,
And chains about your neck.

PROVERBS 1:8–9

Hear, my children, the instruction of a father,
And give attention to know understanding;
For I give you good doctrine:
Do not forsake my law.
When I was my father's son,
Tender and the only one in the sight of my mother,
He also taught me, and said to me:
"Let your heart retain my words;
Keep my commands, and live."

PROVERBS 4:1–4

The fear of the LORD is the beginning of wisdom,
And the knowledge of the Holy One is understanding.
For by me your days will be multiplied,
And years of life will be added to you.

PROVERBS 9:10–11

He who heeds the word wisely will find good,
And whoever trusts in the LORD, happy is he.

PROVERBS 16:20

Honor your father and your mother, that your days may be long upon the land which the LORD your God is giving you.

EXODUS 20:12

Children, obey your parents in the Lord, for this is right. "Honor your father and mother," which is the first commandment with promise: "that it may be well with you and you may live long on the earth."

EPHESIANS 6:1–3

Children, obey your parents in all things, for this is well pleasing to the Lord.

COLOSSIANS 3:20

Likewise you younger people, submit yourselves to your elders. Yes, all of you be submissive to one another, and be clothed with humility, for

"God resists the proud,
But gives grace to the humble."

1 PETER 5:5

WHAT JESUS
MEANS TO YOU...

- His Death
- His Deity
- His Humanity
- His Resurrection
- His Second Coming
- His Love
- His Security
- His Fellowship

HIS DEATH

For He made Him who knew no sin to be sin for us,
that we might become the righteousness of God in Him.

2 CORINTHIANS 5:21

For Christ also suffered once for sins, the just for the
unjust, that He might bring us to God, being put to
death in the flesh but made alive by the Spirit.

1 PETER 3:18

Jesus, knowing that all things were now accomplished,
that the Scripture might be fulfilled, said, "I thirst!"
Now a vessel full of sour wine was sitting there; and they
filled a sponge with sour wine, put it on hyssop, and put
it to His mouth. So when Jesus had received the sour
wine, He said, "It is finished!" And bowing His head, He
gave up His spirit.

JOHN 19:28–30

"Who committed no sin,
  Nor was deceit found in His mouth";
  who, when He was reviled, did not revile in return;
when He suffered, He did not threaten, but committed
Himself to Him who judges righteously; who Himself
bore our sins in His own body on the tree, that we,
having died to sins, might live for righteousness—by
those stripes you were healed.

1 PETER 2:22–24

For when we were still without strength, in due time Christ died for the ungodly. For scarcely for a righteous man will one die; yet perhaps for a good man someone would even dare to die. But God demonstrates His own love toward us, in that while we were still sinners, Christ died for us.

ROMANS 5:6–8

He Himself is the propitiation for our sins, and not for ours only but also for the whole world.

1 JOHN 2:2

HIS DEITY

He is the image of the invisible God, the firstborn over all creation. For by Him all things were created that are in heaven and that are on earth, visible and invisible, whether thrones or dominions or principalities or powers. All things were created through Him and for Him. And He is before all things, and in Him all things consist. And He is the head of the body, the church, who is the beginning, the firstborn from the dead, that in all things He may have the preeminence.

For it pleased the Father that in Him all the fullness should dwell, and by Him to reconcile all things to Himself, by Him, whether things on earth or things in heaven, having made peace through the blood of His cross.

COLOSSIANS 1:15–20

In the beginning was the Word, and the Word was with God, the Word was God. He was in the beginning with God. All things were made through Him, and without Him nothing was made that was made.

JOHN 1:1–3

Yet for us there is one God, the Father, of whom are all things, and we for Him; and one Lord Jesus Christ, through whom are all things, and through whom we live.

1 CORINTHIANS 8:6

"And I give them eternal life, and they shall never perish; neither shall anyone snatch them out of My hand. My Father, who has given them to Me, is greater than all; and no one is able to snatch them out of My Father's hand. I and My Father are one."

JOHN 10:28–30

Looking for the blessed hope and glorious appearing of our great God and Savior Jesus Christ.

TITUS 2:13

My little children, these things I write to you, so that you may not sin. And if anyone sins, we have an Advocate with the Father, Jesus Christ the righteous. And He Himself is the propitiation for our sins, and not for ours only but also for the whole world.

1 JOHN 2:1–2

Who is he who overcomes the world, but he who believes that Jesus is the Son of God?

1 JOHN 5:5

HIS HUMANITY

Then the angel said to her, "Do not be afraid, Mary, for you have found favor with God. And behold, you will conceive in your womb and bring forth a Son, and shall call His name JESUS. He will be great, and will be called the Son of the Highest; and the Lord God will give Him the throne of His father David. And He will reign over the house of Jacob forever, and of His kingdom there will be no end."

LUKE 1:30–33

[Jesus], being in the form of God, did not consider it robbery to be equal with God, but made Himself of no reputation, taking the form of a bondservant, and coming in the likeness of men. And being found in appearance as a man, He humbled Himself and became obedient to the point of death, even the death of the cross.

PHILIPPIANS 2:6–8

But as many as received Him, to them He gave the right to become children of God, to those who believe in His name.

JOHN 1:12

For we do not have a High Priest who cannot sympathize with our weaknesses, but was in all points tempted as we are, yet without sin.

HEBREWS 4:15

The Word became flesh and dwelt among us, and we beheld His glory, the glory as of the only begotten of the Father, full of grace and truth.

JOHN 1:14

But when the fullness of the time had come, God sent forth His Son, born of a woman, born under the law, to redeem those who were under the law, that we might receive the adoption as sons.

GALATIANS 4:4–5

HIS RESURRECTION

But He, because He continues forever, has an unchangeable priesthood. Therefore He is also able to save to the uttermost those who come to God through Him, since He always lives to make intercession for them.

HEBREWS 7:24–25

I delivered to you first of all that which I also received: that Christ died for our sins according to the Scriptures, and that He was buried, and that He rose again the third day according to the Scriptures, and that He was seen by Cephas, then by the twelve. After that He was seen by over five hundred brethren at once, of whom the greater part remain to the present, but some have fallen asleep. After that He was seen by James, then by all the apostles. Then last of all He was seen by me also, as by one born out of due time.

1 CORINTHIANS 15:3–8

And He is the head of the body, the church, who is the beginning, the firstborn from the dead, that in all things He may have the preeminence.

COLOSSIANS 1:18

But the angel answered and said to the women, "Do not be afraid, for I know that you seek Jesus who was crucified. He is not here; for He is risen, as He said. Come, see the place where the Lord lay."

MATTHEW 28:5–6

After he [Jesus] said this, he was taken up before their very eyes, and a cloud hid him from their sight.

ACTS 1:9 NIV

"I am He who lives, and was dead, and behold, I am alive forevermore. Amen. And I have the keys of Hades and of Death."

REVELATION 1:18

HIS SECOND COMING

The Lord Himself will descend from heaven with a shout, with the voice of an archangel, and with the trumpet of God. And the dead in Christ will rise first. Then we who are alive and remain shall be caught up together with them in the clouds to meet the Lord in the air. And thus we shall always be with the Lord. Therefore comfort one another with these words.

1 Thessalonians 4:16–18

"In My Father's house are many mansions; if it were not so, I would have told you. I go to prepare a place for you. And if I go and prepare a place for you, I will come again and receive you to Myself; that where I am, there you may be also."

John 14:2–3

"Be ready, for the Son of Man is coming at an hour you do not expect."

Matthew 24:44

But, beloved, do not forget this one thing, that with the Lord one day is as a thousand years, and a thousand years as one day. The Lord is not slack concerning His promise, as some count slackness, but is longsuffering toward us, not willing that any should perish but that all should come to repentance.

2 Peter 3:8–9

You are all sons of light and sons of the day. We are not of the night nor of darkness. Therefore let us not sleep, as others do, but let us watch and be sober.

1 Thessalonians 5:5–6

They were looking intently up into the sky as he was going, when suddenly two men dressed in white stood beside them. "Men of Galilee," they said, "Why do you stand there looking into the sky? This same Jesus, who has been taken from you into heaven, will come back in the same way you have seen him go into heaven."

Acts 1:10–11 NIV

WHAT JESUS MEANS TO YOU. . .
HIS LOVE

God demonstrates His own love toward us, in that while we were still sinners, Christ died for us.

ROMANS 5:8

"For God so loved the world that He gave His only begotten Son, that whoever believes in Him should not perish but have everlasting life."

JOHN 3:16

Beloved, let us love one another, for love is of God; and everyone who loves is born of God and knows God. He who does not love does not know God, for God is love. In this the love of God was manifested toward us, that God has sent His only begotten Son into the world, that we might live through Him. In this is love, not that we loved God, but that He loved us and sent His Son to be the propitiation for our sins. Beloved, if God so loved us, we also ought to love one another. No one has seen God at any time. If we love one another, God abides in us, and His love has been perfected in us.

1 JOHN 4:7–12

And we have known and believed the love that God has for us. God is love, and he who abides in love abides in God, and God in him. . . . We love Him because He first loved us.

1 JOHN 4:16, 19

"As the Father loved Me, I also have loved you; abide in My love. If you keep My commandments, you will abide in My love, just as I have kept My Father's commandments and abide in His love. These things I have spoken to you, that My joy may remain in you, and that your joy may be full. This is My commandment, that you love one another as I have loved you. Greater love has no one than this, than to lay down one's life for his friends."

JOHN 15:9–13

That Christ may dwell in your hearts through faith; that you, being rooted and grounded in love, may be able to comprehend with all the saints what is the width and length and depth and height—to know the love of Christ which passes knowledge; that you may be filled with all the fullness of God.

EPHESIANS 3:17–19

I love those who love me,
And those who seek me diligently will find me.

PROVERBS 8:17

"He who has My commandments and keeps them, it is he who loves Me. And he who loves Me will be loved by My Father, and I will love him and manifest Myself to him."

JOHN 14:21

Now before the Feast of the Passover, when Jesus knew that His hour had come that He should depart from this world to the Father, having loved His own who were in the world, He loved them to the end.

JOHN 13:1

For I am persuaded that neither death nor life, nor angels nor principalities nor powers, nor things present nor things to come, nor height nor depth, nor any other created thing, shall be able to separate us from the love of God which is in Christ Jesus our Lord.

ROMANS 8:38–39

HIS SECURITY

Blessed be the God and Father of our Lord Jesus Christ, who according to His abundant mercy has begotten us again to a living hope through the resurrection of Jesus Christ from the dead, to an inheritance incorruptible and undefiled and that does not fade away, reserved in heaven for you, who are kept by the power of God through faith for salvation ready to be revealed in the last time.

1 PETER 1:3–5

"My sheep hear My voice, and I know them, and they follow Me. And I give them eternal life, and they shall never perish; neither shall anyone snatch them out of My hand. My Father, who has given them to Me, is greater than all; and no one is able to snatch them out of My Father's hand. I and My Father are one."

JOHN 10:27–30

Being confident of this very thing, that He who has begun a good work in you will complete it until the day of Jesus Christ.

PHILIPPIANS 1:6

The Lord is faithful, who will establish you and guard you from the evil one.

2 THESSALONIANS 3:3

Now to Him who is able to keep you from stumbling,
And to present you faultless
Before the presence of His glory with exceeding joy,
To God our Savior,
Who alone is wise,
Be glory and majesty,
Dominion and power,
Both now and forever.
Amen.

JUDE VV. 24–25

Lift up your eyes on high,
And see who has created these things,
Who brings out their host by number;
He calls them all by name,
By the greatness of His might
And the strength of His power;
Not one is missing.

ISAIAH 40:26

"Do not labor for the food which perishes, but for the food which endures to everlasting life, which the Son of Man will give you, because God the Father has set His seal on Him."

JOHN 6:27

Now to Him who is able to establish you according to my gospel and the preaching of Jesus Christ . . . to God, alone wise, be glory through Jesus Christ forever. Amen.

ROMANS 16:25, 27

In Him you also trusted, after you heard the word of truth, the gospel of your salvation; in whom also, having believed, you were sealed with the Holy Spirit of promise, who is the guarantee of our inheritance until the redemption of the purchased possession, to the praise of His glory.

EPHESIANS 1:13–14

Now it is God who makes both us and you stand firm in Christ. He anointed us, set his seal of ownership on us, and put his Spirit in our hearts as a deposit, guaranteeing what is to come.

2 CORINTHIANS 1:21–22

HIS FELLOWSHIP

That which we have seen and heard we declare to you, that you also may have fellowship with us; and truly our fellowship is with the Father and with His Son Jesus Christ.

1 JOHN 1:3

God is faithful, by whom you were called into the fellowship of His Son, Jesus Christ our Lord.

1 CORINTHIANS 1:9

"Behold, I stand at the door and knock. If anyone hears My voice and opens the door, I will come in to him and dine with him, and he with Me."

REVELATION 3:20

Jesus answered and said to him, "If anyone loves Me, he will keep My word; and My Father will love him, and We will come to him and make Our home with him."

JOHN 14:23

"He who has My commandments and keeps them, it is he who loves Me. And he who loves Me will be loved by My Father, and I will love him and manifest Myself to him."

JOHN 14:21

"Where two or three are gathered together in My name, I am there in the midst of them."

MATTHEW 18:20

"Abide in Me, and I in you. As the branch cannot bear fruit of itself, unless it abides in the vine, neither can you, unless you abide in Me. I am the vine, you are the branches. He who abides in Me, and I in him, bears much fruit; for without Me you can do nothing. . . . If you abide in Me, and My words abide in you, you will ask what you desire, and it shall be done for you."

JOHN 15:4–5, 7

Walk in love, as Christ also has loved us and given Himself for us, an offering and a sacrifice to God for a sweet-smelling aroma. . . . Speaking to one another in psalms and hymns and spiritual songs, singing and making melody in your heart to the Lord. . . . For we are members of His body, of His flesh and of His bones.

EPHESIANS 5:2, 19, 30

This is the message which we have heard from Him and declare to you, that God is light and in Him is no darkness at all. If we say that we have fellowship with Him, and walk in darkness, we lie and do not practice the truth. But if we walk in the light as He is in the light, we have fellowship with one another, and the blood of Jesus Christ His Son cleanses us from all sin.

1 JOHN 1:5–7

WHAT TO DO WHEN YOU ARE...

- Afraid
- Developing Bad Habits
- Lying
- In Need of Prayer
- Seeking God's Will
- Suffering
- Doubting
- Making Bad Choices
- Uncertain About God
- Totally Down

AFRAID

God has not given us a spirit of fear, but of power and of love and of a sound mind.

2 TIMOTHY 1:7

You did not receive the spirit of bondage again to fear, but you received the Spirit of adoption by whom we cry out, "Abba, Father." The Spirit Himself bears witness with our spirit that we are children of God.

ROMANS 8:15–16

I will both lie down in peace, and sleep;
For You alone, O LORD, make me dwell in safety.

PSALM 4:8

He who dwells in the secret place of the Most High
Shall abide under the shadow of the Almighty.
I will say of the LORD, "He is my refuge and my
  fortress;
My God, in Him I will trust."

PSALM 91:1–2

But those who wait on the LORD
Shall renew their strength;
They shall mount up with wings like eagles,
They shall run and not be weary,
They shall walk and not faint.

ISAIAH 40:31

So we may boldly say:
"The LORD is my helper;
I will not fear.
What can man do to me?"

HEBREWS 13:6

Yea, though I walk through the valley of the shadow
  of death,
I will fear no evil;
For You are with me;
Your rod and Your staff, they comfort me.
You prepare a table before me in the presence of my enemies;
You anoint my head with oil;
My cup runs over.

PSALM 23:4–5

The LORD is my light and my salvation;
Whom shall I fear?
The LORD is the strength of my life;
Of whom shall I be afraid? . . .
Though an army may encamp against me,
My heart shall not fear;
Though war may rise against me,
In this I will be confident.

PSALM 27:1, 3

There is no fear in love; but perfect love casts out fear,
because fear involves torment. But he who fears has not
been made perfect in love.

1 JOHN 4:18

DEVELOPING BAD HABITS

Whatever things are true, whatever things are noble, whatever things are just, whatever things are pure, whatever things are lovely, whatever things are of good report, if there is any virtue and if there is anything praiseworthy—meditate on these things. The things which you learned and received and heard and saw in me, these do, and the God of peace will be with you.

PHILIPPIANS 4:8–9

I can do all things through Christ who strengthens me.

PHILIPPIANS 4:13

Your word I have hidden in my heart,
That I might not sin against You.

PSALM 119:11

Therefore submit to God. Resist the devil and he will flee from you. Draw near to God and He will draw near to you.

JAMES 4:7–8

Now may our Lord Jesus Christ Himself, and our God and Father, who has loved us and given us everlasting consolation and good hope by grace, comfort your hearts and establish you in every good word and work.

2 THESSALONIANS 2:16–17

I beseech you therefore, brethren, by the mercies of God, that you present your bodies a living sacrifice, holy, acceptable to God, which is your reasonable service. And do not be conformed to this world, but be transformed by the renewing of your mind, that you may prove what is that good and acceptable and perfect will of God.

ROMANS 12:1–2

Then He said to them all, "If anyone desires to come after Me, let him deny himself, and take up his cross daily, and follow Me."

LUKE 9:23

I have been crucified with Christ; it is no longer I who live, but Christ lives in me; and the life which I now live in the flesh I live by faith in the Son of God, who loved me and gave Himself for me.

GALATIANS 2:20

Be diligent to present yourself approved to God, a worker who does not need to be ashamed, rightly dividing the word of truth.

2 TIMOTHY 2:15

LYING

Wash me thoroughly from my iniquity,
And cleanse me from my sin. . . .
Behold, You desire truth in the inward parts,
And in the hidden part You will make me to know
  wisdom.

PSALM 51:2, 6

These are the things you shall do:
Speak each man the truth to his neighbor;
Give judgment in your gates for truth, justice, and peace;
Let none of you think evil in your heart against
  your neighbor;
And do not love a false oath.

ZECHARIAH 8:16–17

Lying lips are an abomination to the LORD,
But those who deal truthfully are His delight.

PROVERBS 12:22

Do not lie to one another, since you have put off the
old man with his deeds.

COLOSSIANS 3:9

"Let your 'Yes' be 'Yes,' and your 'No,' 'No.' For
whatever is more than these is from the evil one."

MATTHEW 5:37

Who is the man who desires life,
And loves many days, that he may see good?
Keep your tongue from evil,
And your lips from speaking deceit.

PSALM 34:12–13

Let the words of my mouth and the meditation
    of my heart
Be acceptable in Your sight,
O LORD, my strength and my Redeemer.

PSALM 19:14

Therefore let us pursue the things which make for
peace and the things by which one may edify another.

ROMANS 14:19

Pursue peace with all people, and holiness, without
which no one will see the Lord.

HEBREWS 12:14

IN NEED OF PRAYER

Be anxious for nothing, but in everything by prayer and supplication, with thanksgiving, let your requests be made known to God; and the peace of God, which surpasses all understanding, will guard your hearts and minds through Christ Jesus.

PHILIPPIANS 4:6–7

"Ask, and it will be given to you; seek, and you will find; knock, and it will be opened to you. For everyone who asks receives, and he who seeks finds, and to him who knocks it will be opened."

MATTHEW 7:7–8

Confess your trespasses to one another, and pray for one another, that you may be healed. The effective, fervent prayer of a righteous man avails much.

JAMES 5:16

Praying always with all prayer and supplication in the Spirit, being watchful to this end with all perseverance and supplication for all the saints.

EPHESIANS 6:18

Now this is the confidence that we have in Him, that if we ask anything according to His will, He hears us.

1 JOHN 5:14

I cried to Him with my mouth,
And He was extolled with my tongue.
If I regard iniquity in my heart,
The Lord will not hear.
But certainly God has heard me;
He has attended to the voice of my prayer.
Blessed be God,
Who has not turned away my prayer,
Nor His mercy from me!

PSALM 66:17–20

Call to Me, and I will answer you, and show you great
and mighty things, which you do not know.

JEREMIAH 33:3

SEEKING GOD'S WILL

Do not be conformed to this world, but be transformed by the renewing of your mind, that you may prove what is that good and acceptable and perfect will of God.

ROMANS 12:2

A man's heart plans his way,
But the LORD directs his steps.

PROVERBS 16:9

Trust in the LORD with all your heart,
And lean not on your own understanding;
In all your ways acknowledge Him,
And He shall direct your paths.

PROVERBS 3:5–6

Your word is a lamp to my feet
And a light to my path.

PSALM 119:105

Delight yourself also in the LORD,
And He shall give you the desires of your heart.

PSALM 37:4

The steps of a good man are ordered by the LORD,
And He delights in his way.

PSALM 37:23

I will instruct you and teach you in the way you
   should go;
I will guide you with My eye.

PSALM 32:8

For I know the thoughts that I think toward you, says
the LORD, thoughts of peace and not of evil, to give you a
future and a hope. Then you will call upon Me and go and
pray to Me, and I will listen to you. And you will seek Me
and find Me, when you search for Me with all your heart.

JEREMIAH 29:11–13

The LORD leads with unfailing love and faithfulness
all who keep his covenant and obey his demands.

PSALM 25:10 NLT

SUFFERING

My brethren, count it all joy when you fall into various trials, knowing that the testing of your faith produces patience. But let patience have its perfect work, that you may be perfect and complete, lacking nothing.

JAMES 1:2–4

Beloved, do not think it strange concerning the fiery trial which is to try you, as though some strange thing happened to you; but rejoice to the extent that you partake of Christ's sufferings, that when His glory is revealed, you may also be glad with exceeding joy.

1 PETER 4:12–13

For our light affliction, which is but for a moment, is working for us a far more exceeding and eternal weight of glory.

2 CORINTHIANS 4:17

The Spirit Himself bears witness with our spirit that we are children of God, and if children, then heirs— heirs of God and joint heirs with Christ, if indeed we suffer with Him, that we may also be glorified together. For I consider that the sufferings of this present time are not worthy to be compared with the glory which shall be revealed in us.

ROMANS 8:16–18

We also glory in tribulations, knowing that tribulation produces perseverance; and perseverance, character; and character, hope. Now hope does not disappoint, because the love of God has been poured out in our hearts by the Holy Spirit who was given to us.

ROMANS 5:3–5

Is anyone among you suffering? Let him pray. Is anyone cheerful? Let him sing psalms. Is anyone among you sick? Let him call for the elders of the church, and let them pray over him, anointing him with oil in the name of the Lord.

JAMES 5:13–14

But thanks be to God, who gives us the victory through our Lord Jesus Christ. Therefore, my beloved brethren, be steadfast, immovable, always abounding in the work of the Lord, knowing that your labor is not in vain in the Lord.

1 CORINTHIANS 15:57–58

Call upon Me in the day of trouble;
I will deliver you, and you shall glorify Me.

PSALM 50:15

DOUBTING YOURSELF

Fear not, for I am with you;
Be not dismayed, for I am your God.
I will strengthen you,
Yes, I will help you,
I will uphold you with My righteous right hand.

ISAIAH 41:10

For the Lord GOD will help Me;
Therefore I will not be disgraced;
Therefore I have set My face like a flint,
And I know that I will not be ashamed.

ISAIAH 50:7

Cast your burden on the LORD,
And He shall sustain you;
He shall never permit the righteous to be moved.

PSALM 55:22

For we are His workmanship, created in Christ Jesus
for good works, which God prepared beforehand that
we should walk in them.

EPHESIANS 2:10

For God is not the author of confusion but of peace.

1 CORINTHIANS 14:33

Therefore it is also contained in the Scripture,
"Behold, I lay in Zion
A chief cornerstone, elect, precious,
And he who believes on Him will by no means be put
  to shame."

1 PETER 2:6

When you pass through the waters, I will be with you;
And through the rivers, they shall not overflow you.
When you walk through the fire, you shall not be
  burned,
Nor shall the flame scorch you.

ISAIAH 43:2

Now may the God of peace . . . make you complete in
every good work to do His will, working in you what is well
pleasing in His sight, through Jesus Christ, to whom be glory
forever and ever. Amen.

HEBREWS 13:20–21

For I am persuaded that neither death nor life, nor
angels nor principalities nor powers, nor things present
nor things to come, nor height nor depth, nor any other
created thing, shall be able to separate us from the love
of God which is in Christ Jesus our Lord.

ROMANS 8:38–39

MAKING BAD CHOICES

If we confess our sins, He is faithful and just to forgive us our sins and to cleanse us from all unrighteousness. If we say that we have not sinned, we make Him a liar, and His word is not in us.

1 John 1:9–10

Therefore you shall be careful to do as the Lord your God has commanded you; you shall not turn aside to the right hand or to the left. You shall walk in all the ways which the Lord your God has commanded you, that you may live and that it may be well with you, and that you may prolong your days in the land which you shall possess.

Deuteronomy 5:32–33

Do not be conformed to this world, but be transformed by the renewing of your mind, that you may prove what is that good and acceptable and perfect will of God.

Romans 12:2

I will heal their backsliding,
I will love them freely,
For My anger has turned away from him.

Hosea 14:4

The way of the just is uprightness;
O Most Upright,
You weigh the path of the just.

ISAIAH 26:7

Let integrity and uprightness preserve me,
For I wait for You.

PSALM 25:21

Therefore we also, since we are surrounded by so great a cloud of witnesses, let us lay aside every weight, and the sin which so easily ensnares us, and let us run with endurance the race that is set before us.

HEBREWS 12:1

When a man's ways please the LORD,
He makes even his enemies to be at peace with him.
Better is a little with righteousness,
Than vast revenues without justice.

PROVERBS 16:7–8

And let us not grow weary while doing good, for in due season we shall reap if we do not lose heart.

GALATIANS 6:9

UNCERTAIN ABOUT GOD

So Jesus answered and said to them, "Have faith in God. For assuredly, I say to you, whoever says to this mountain, 'Be removed and be cast into the sea,' and does not doubt in his heart, but believes that those things he says will be done, he will have whatever he says. Therefore I say to you, whatever things you ask when you pray, believe that you receive them, and you will have them."

MARK 11:22–24

"Do not seek what you should eat or what you should drink, nor have an anxious mind. For all these things the nations of the world seek after, and your Father knows that you need these things. But seek the kingdom of God, and all these things shall be added to you."

LUKE 12:29–31

For as the rain comes down, and the snow from heaven,
And do not return there,
But water the earth,
And make it bring forth and bud,
That it may give seed to the sower
And bread to the eater,
So shall My word be that goes forth from My mouth;
It shall not return to Me void,
But it shall accomplish what I please,
And it shall prosper in the thing for which I sent it.

ISAIAH 55:10–11

For I am God, and there is no other;
I am God, and there is none like Me,
Declaring the end from the beginning,
And from ancient times things that are not yet done,
Saying, "My counsel shall stand,
And I will do all My pleasure."

ISAIAH 46:9–10

Now may the God of peace Himself sanctify you completely; and may your whole spirit, soul, and body be preserved blameless at the coming of our Lord Jesus Christ. He who calls you is faithful, who also will do it.

1 THESSALONIANS 5:23–24

The Lord is not slack concerning His promise, as some count slackness, but is longsuffering toward us, not willing that any should perish but that all should come to repentance.

2 PETER 3:9

"For the mountains shall depart
And the hills be removed,
But My kindness shall not depart from you,
Nor shall My covenant of peace be removed,"
Says the LORD, who has mercy on you.

ISAIAH 54:10

And we know that all things work together for good to those who love God, to those who are the called according to His purpose.

ROMANS 8:28

TOTALLY DOWN

You will keep him in perfect peace,
Whose mind is stayed on You,
Because he trusts in You.
Trust in the LORD forever,
For in YAH, the LORD, is everlasting strength.

ISAIAH 26:3–4

But if the Spirit of Him who raised Jesus from the
dead dwells in you, He who raised Christ from the dead
will also give life to your mortal bodies through His
Spirit who dwells in you.

ROMANS 8:11

Having been justified by faith, we have peace with
God through our Lord Jesus Christ, through whom
also we have access by faith into this grace in which we
stand, and rejoice in hope of the glory of God.

ROMANS 5:1–2

For it is the God who commanded light to shine out of
darkness, who has shone in our hearts to give the light
of the knowledge of the glory of God in the face of Jesus
Christ. . . . We are hard pressed on every side, yet not
crushed; we are perplexed, but not in despair; persecuted,
but not forsaken; struck down, but not destroyed.

2 CORINTHIANS 4:6, 8–9

He will swallow up death forever,
And the Lord God will wipe away tears from all faces;
The rebuke of His people
He will take away from all the earth;
For the Lord has spoken.
And it will be said in that day:
"Behold, this is our God;
We have waited for Him, and He will save us.
This is the Lord;
We have waited for Him;
We will be glad and rejoice in His salvation."

ISAIAH 25:8–9

But the salvation of the righteous is from the Lord;
He is their strength in the time of trouble.
And the Lord shall help them and deliver them;
He shall deliver them from the wicked,
And save them,
Because they trust in Him.

PSALM 37:39–40

"Peace I leave with you, My peace I give to you; not as the world gives do I give to you. Let not your heart be troubled, neither let it be afraid."

JOHN 14:27

Now may the God of hope fill you with all joy and peace in believing, that you may abound in hope by the power of the Holy Spirit.

ROMANS 15:13

TRUTH FROM THE
BIBLE ABOUT...

- Christian Fellowship
- Your Responsibility
- God's Will for Your Life
- Answered Prayer
- Speaking God's Word
- Forgiving Others
- God's Plan of Salvation

CHRISTIAN FELLOWSHIP

That which we have seen and heard we declare to you, that you also may have fellowship with us; and truly our fellowship is with the Father and with His Son Jesus Christ. . . . But if we walk in the light as He is in the light, we have fellowship with one another, and the blood of Jesus Christ His Son cleanses us from all sin.

1 JOHN 1:3, 7

Walk in love, as Christ also has loved us and given Himself for us, an offering and a sacrifice to God for a sweet-smelling aroma . . . speaking to one another in psalms and hymns and spiritual songs, singing and making melody in your heart to the Lord, giving thanks always for all things to God the Father in the name of our Lord Jesus Christ.

EPHESIANS 5:2, 19–20

Now, therefore, you are no longer strangers and foreigners, but fellow citizens with the saints and members of the household of God, having been built on the foundation of the apostles and prophets, Jesus Christ Himself being the chief cornerstone, in whom the whole building, being fitted together, grows into a holy temple in the Lord, in whom you also are being built together for a dwelling place of God in the Spirit.

EPHESIANS 2:19–22

Let the word of Christ dwell in you richly in all wisdom, teaching and admonishing one another in psalms and hymns and spiritual songs, singing with grace in your hearts to the Lord. And whatever you do in word or deed, do all in the name of the Lord Jesus, giving thanks to God the Father through Him.

COLOSSIANS 3:16–17

That their hearts may be encouraged, being knit together in love, and attaining to all riches of the full assurance of understanding, to the knowledge of the mystery of God, both of the Father and of Christ.

COLOSSIANS 2:2

For you are a holy people to the LORD your God; the LORD your God has chosen you to be a people for Himself, a special treasure above all the peoples on the face of the earth.

DEUTERONOMY 7:6

Therefore if there is any consolation in Christ, if any comfort of love, if any fellowship of the Spirit, if any affection and mercy, fulfill my joy by being like-minded, having the same love, being of one accord, of one mind.

PHILIPPIANS 2:1–2

Now I plead with you, brethren, by the name of our Lord Jesus Christ, that you all speak the same thing, and that there be no divisions among you, but that you be perfectly joined together in the same mind and in the same judgment.

1 CORINTHIANS 1:10

Now may the God of patience and comfort grant you to be like-minded toward one another, according to Christ Jesus, that you may with one mind and one mouth glorify the God and Father of our Lord Jesus Christ. Therefore receive one another, just as Christ also received us, to the glory of God.

ROMANS 15:5–7

Let us draw near with a true heart in full assurance of faith, having our hearts sprinkled from an evil conscience and our bodies washed with pure water. Let us hold fast the confession of our hope without wavering, for He who promised is faithful. And let us consider one another in order to stir up love and good works, not forsaking the assembling of ourselves together, as is the manner of some, but exhorting one another, and so much the more as you see the Day approaching.

HEBREWS 10:22–25

YOUR RESPONSIBILITY

"You shall receive power when the Holy Spirit has come upon you; and you shall be witnesses to Me in Jerusalem, and in all Judea and Samaria, and to the end of the earth."

ACTS 1:8

"You are the light of the world. A city that is set on a hill cannot be hidden. Nor do they light a lamp and put it under a basket, but on a lampstand, and it gives light to all who are in the house. Let your light so shine before men, that they may see your good works and glorify your Father in heaven."

MATTHEW 5:14–16

Bear one another's burdens, and so fulfill the law of Christ. . . . Let him who is taught the word share in all good things with him who teaches.

GALATIANS 6:2, 6

By this we know love, because He laid down His life for us. And we also ought to lay down our lives for the brethren. But whoever has this world's goods, and sees his brother in need, and shuts up his heart from him, how does the love of God abide in him? My little children, let us not love in word or in tongue, but in deed and in truth.

1 JOHN 3:16–18

Whatever we ask we receive from Him, because we keep His commandments and do those things that are pleasing in His sight. And this is His commandment: that we should believe on the name of His Son Jesus Christ and love one another, as He gave us commandment.

1 John 3:22–23

You shall lay up these words of mine in your heart and in your soul, and bind them as a sign on your hand, and they shall be as frontlets between your eyes. You shall teach them to your children, speaking of them when you sit in your house, when you walk by the way, when you lie down, and when you rise up.

Deuteronomy 11:18–19

My son, keep your father's command,
And do not forsake the law of your mother. . . .
When you roam, they will lead you;
When you sleep, they will keep you;
And when you awake, they will speak with you.
For the commandment is a lamp,
And the law a light;
Reproofs of instruction are the way of life.

Proverbs 6:20, 22–23

You shall love the LORD your God, and keep His charge, His statutes, His judgments, and His commandments always.

Deuteronomy 11:1

"Go into all the world and preach the gospel to every creature."

MARK 16:15

This Book of the Law shall not depart from your mouth, but you shall meditate in it day and night, that you may observe to do according to all that is written in it. For then you will make your way prosperous, and then you will have good success. Have I not commanded you? Be strong and of good courage; do not be afraid, nor be dismayed, for the LORD your God is with you wherever you go.

JOSHUA 1:8–9

GOD'S WILL FOR YOUR LIFE

If any of you lacks wisdom, let him ask of God, who gives to all liberally and without reproach, and it will be given to him.

JAMES 1:5

The LORD leads with unfailing love and faithfulness all who keep his covenant and obey his demands.

PSALM 25:10 NLT

Your word is a lamp to my feet
And a light to my path.
I have sworn and confirmed
That I will keep Your righteous judgments.

PSALM 119:105–106

Your ears shall hear a word behind you, saying,
"This is the way, walk in it,"
Whenever you turn to the right hand
Or whenever you turn to the left.

ISAIAH 30:21

See then that you walk circumspectly, not as fools but as wise, redeeming the time, because the days are evil. Therefore do not be unwise, but understand what the will of the Lord is.

EPHESIANS 5:15–17

Rejoice always, pray without ceasing, in everything give thanks; for this is the will of God in Christ Jesus for you.

1 THESSALONIANS 5:16–18

Teach me to do Your will,
For You are my God;
Your Spirit is good.
Lead me in the land of uprightness.

PSALM 143:10

My son, do not forget my law,
But let your heart keep my commands. . . .
Trust in the LORD with all your heart,
And lean not on your own understanding;
In all your ways acknowledge Him,
And He shall direct your paths. . . .
My son, do not despise the chastening of the LORD,
Nor detest His correction;
For whom the LORD loves He corrects,
Just as a father the son in whom he delights.

PROVERBS 3:1, 5–6, 11–12

ANSWERED PRAYER

"Ask, and it will be given to you; seek, and you will find; knock, and it will be opened to you. For everyone who asks receives, and he who seeks finds, and to him who knocks it will be opened."

MATTHEW 7:7–8

"Again I say to you that if two of you agree on earth concerning anything that they ask, it will be done for them by My Father in heaven. For where two or three are gathered together in My name, I am there in the midst of them."

MATTHEW 18:19–20

Whatever we ask we receive from Him, because we keep His commandments and do those things that are pleasing in His sight. And this is His commandment: that we should believe on the name of His Son Jesus Christ and love one another, as He gave us commandment. Now he who keeps His commandments abides in Him, and He in him. And by this we know that He abides in us, by the Spirit whom He has given us.

1 JOHN 3:22–24

Let us therefore come boldly to the throne of grace, that we may obtain mercy and find grace to help in time of need.

HEBREWS 4:16

"Therefore I say to you, whatever things you ask when you pray, believe that you receive them, and you will have them. And whenever you stand praying, if you have anything against anyone, forgive him, that your Father in heaven may also forgive you your trespasses."

MARK 11:24–25

"Whatever you ask in My name, that I will do, that the Father may be glorified in the Son. If you ask anything in My name, I will do it."

JOHN 14:13–14

"When you pray, go into your room, and when you have shut your door, pray to your Father who is in the secret place; and your Father who sees in secret will reward you openly."

MATTHEW 6:6

He shall call upon Me, and I will answer him;
I will be with him in trouble;
I will deliver him and honor him.
With long life I will satisfy him,
And show him My salvation.

PSALM 91:15–16

Thus says the LORD who made it, the LORD who formed it to establish it (the LORD is His name): "Call to Me, and I will answer you, and show you great and mighty things, which you do not know."

JEREMIAH 33:2–3

SPEAKING GOD'S WORD

"For assuredly, I say to you, whoever says to this mountain, 'Be removed and be cast into the sea,' and does not doubt in his heart, but believes that those things he says will be done, he will have whatever he says."

MARK 11:23

"If you have faith as a mustard seed, you can say to this mulberry tree, 'Be pulled up by the roots and be planted in the sea,' and it would obey you."

LUKE 17:6

But what does it say? "The word is near you, in your mouth and in your heart" (that is, the word of faith which we preach): that if you confess with your mouth the Lord Jesus and believe in your heart that God has raised Him from the dead, you will be saved. For with the heart one believes unto righteousness, and with the mouth confession is made unto salvation.

ROMANS 10:8–10

Since we have the same spirit of faith, according to what is written, "I believed and therefore I spoke," we also believe and therefore speak, knowing that He who raised up the Lord Jesus will also raise us up with Jesus, and will present us with you.

2 CORINTHIANS 4:13–14

Speaking the truth in love, [we] may grow up in all things into Him who is the head—Christ.

EPHESIANS 4:15

The wise in heart will be called prudent,
And sweetness of the lips increases learning. . . .
The heart of the wise teaches his mouth,
And adds learning to his lips.
Pleasant words are like a honeycomb,
Sweetness to the soul and health to the bones.

PROVERBS 16:21, 23–24

The words of a man's mouth are deep waters;
The wellspring of wisdom is a flowing brook. . . .
Death and life are in the power of the tongue,
And those who love it will eat its fruit.

PROVERBS 18:4, 21

"Therefore whoever confesses Me before men, him I will also confess before My Father who is in heaven."

MATTHEW 10:32

Let us hold fast the confession of our hope without wavering, for He who promised is faithful.

HEBREWS 10:23

For I am not ashamed of the gospel of Christ, for it is the power of God to salvation for everyone who believes, for the Jew first and also for the Greek.

ROMANS 1:16

FORGIVING OTHERS

"If you forgive men their trespasses, your heavenly Father will also forgive you. But if you do not forgive men their trespasses, neither will your Father forgive your trespasses."

MATTHEW 6:14–15

Then Peter came to Him and said, "Lord, how often shall my brother sin against me, and I forgive him? Up to seven times?"

Jesus said to him, "I do not say to you, up to seven times, but up to seventy times seven."

MATTHEW 18:21–22

"For this is My blood of the new covenant, which is shed for many for the remission of sins."

MATTHEW 26:28

"Whenever you stand praying, if you have anything against anyone, forgive him, that your Father in heaven may also forgive you your trespasses."

MARK 11:25

Bearing with one another, and forgiving one another, if anyone has a complaint against another; even as Christ forgave you, so you also must do.

COLOSSIANS 3:13

Finally, all of you be of one mind, having compassion for one another; love as brothers, be tenderhearted, be courteous; not returning evil for evil or reviling for reviling, but on the contrary blessing, knowing that you were called to this, that you may inherit a blessing.

1 PETER 3:8–9

Let all bitterness, wrath, anger, clamor, and evil speaking be put away from you, with all malice. And be kind to one another, tenderhearted, forgiving one another, even as God in Christ forgave you.

EPHESIANS 4:31–32

So now there is no condemnation for those who belong to Christ Jesus. And because you belong to him, the power of the life-giving Spirit has freed you from the power of sin that leads to death.

ROMANS 8:1–2 NLT

I do not count myself to have apprehended; but one thing I do, forgetting those things which are behind and reaching forward to those things which are ahead, I press toward the goal for the prize of the upward call of God in Christ Jesus.

PHILIPPIANS 3:13–14

"Take heed to yourselves. If your brother sins against you, rebuke him; and if he repents, forgive him. And if he sins against you seven times in a day, and seven times in a day returns to you, saying, 'I repent,' you shall forgive him."

Luke 17:3–4

Do not remember the former things,
Nor consider the things of old. . . .
I, even I, am He who blots out your transgressions for
   My own sake;
And I will not remember your sins.

Isaiah 43:18, 25

GOD'S PLAN OF SALVATION

All have sinned and fall short of the glory of God, being justified freely by His grace through the redemption that is in Christ Jesus.

ROMANS 3:23–24

God demonstrates His own love toward us, in that while we were still sinners, Christ died for us.

ROMANS 5:8

The wages of sin is death, but the gift of God is eternal life in Christ Jesus our Lord.

ROMANS 6:23

But what does it say? "The word is near you, in your mouth and in your heart" (that is, the word of faith which we preach): that if you confess with your mouth the Lord Jesus and believe in your heart that God has raised Him from the dead, you will be saved. For with the heart one believes unto righteousness, and with the mouth confession is made unto salvation.

ROMANS 10:8–10

I declare to you the gospel which I preached to you, which also you received and in which you stand, by which also you are saved, if you hold fast that word which I preached to you—unless you believed in vain. For I delivered to you first of all that which I also received: that Christ died for our sins according to the Scriptures, and that He was buried, and that He rose again the third day according to the Scriptures.

1 CORINTHIANS 15:1–4

"For God so loved the world that He gave His only begotten Son, that whoever believes in Him should not perish but have everlasting life. For God did not send His Son into the world to condemn the world, but that the world through Him might be saved."

JOHN 3:16–17

By grace you have been saved through faith, and that not of yourselves; it is the gift of God, not of works, lest anyone should boast.

EPHESIANS 2:8–9

"Behold, I stand at the door and knock. If anyone hears My voice and opens the door, I will come in to him and dine with him, and he with Me."

REVELATION 3:20

This is the testimony: that God has given us eternal life, and this life is in His Son. He who has the Son has life; he who does not have the Son of God does not have life. These things I have written to you who believe in the name of the Son of God, that you may know that you have eternal life, and that you may continue to believe in the name of the Son of God.

1 JOHN 5:11–13

A FINAL WORD
TO THE GRADUATE

As you continue your adventures on this earth, please remember to carry the promises of God with you. Amid all of life's uncertainty, His Word alone is always true, always reliable. Believe in Him. Study His Word. Live His will. And be confident that someday you'll graduate from this life into a new, perfect one in heaven.

Grace, mercy,
and peace will be with you
from God the Father and
from the Lord Jesus Christ,
the Son of the Father,
in truth and love.

2 JOHN V. 3